Flavors of
JAPAN

ACKNOWLEDGEMENT

This book was made possible with a lot of help from our friends. We'd like especially to thank (alphabetically) Felisa Capillo, Gerry Horiuchi, Takako Ishizaki, Yuriko Kimura, Kayo Kurata, Lana Ninomiya, Setsuko Ohata, Marvin Pettis, Shirley Sasaki—and our mom, Kiyoko Hirasuna, and sister, Pat Oda, who made this a family project.

This book is dedicated
to our mom and dad
Kiyoko and Eddie Hirasuna

Flavors of
JAPAN

Delphine Hirasuna
Diane J. Hirasuna

ILLUSTRATIONS BY SALLY NOLL

101 Productions

Library of Congress Catalog Card Number 88-71977
ISBN 0-89721-167-7

CONTENTS

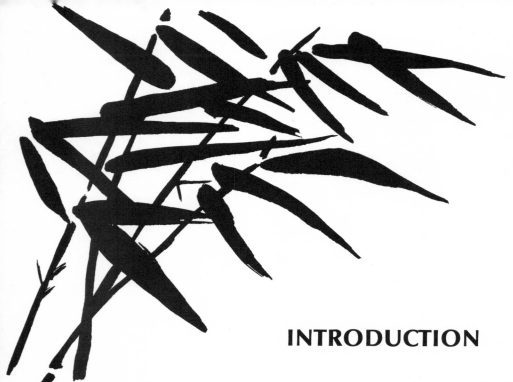

INTRODUCTION

On a visit to Japan a few years ago we stayed with relatives in Hiroshima who are carrying on the century-old family banquet-catering business. One day our second cousins, who run the business from their home, were busy preparing for a large wedding. We offered to help, but soon found that we could help best by staying at a respectful distance and watching.

With knives flashing like twirling batons, they transformed small potatoes *(imo)* into tree mushrooms, raw fish *(sashimi)* into roses in full bloom, and lotus roots *(renkon)* into delightful little umbrellas. Nothing for this feast was carelessly placed on a platter.

The Japanese believe that food should delight the eyes, as well as please the palate. Every cook strives for harmonious colors and lively touches when arranging a meal. Each course is presented separately in small individual portions, both to preserve the purity of flavors and to allow diners to appreciate the total visual image of the dish with the food on it. A dish is looked upon as a picture frame: it enhances the beauty of the food, rather than detracts from it.

As with other Japanese art forms, simplicity and reverence for nature are fundamental qualities of the culinary arts. In this the Japanese were greatly influenced by Zen

Buddhism, which was introduced to Japan from China in the sixth century. Both the ancient Japanese who were nature worshippers and the Zen disciples believed that man should not tamper with nature, but live in harmony with it. The Zen monks, who practiced *shojin ryori* (vegetarian cooking), taught ways of selecting foods grown in their natural environment and of preparing them to bring out the distinct inherent flavors. The Zen followers believed that there was a rhythm to life and to the universe and man was meant to flow with it rather than divert the path to unnatural directions. Part of this thought was that food must be kept within its season, when each is at its plumpest and most abundant.

Even with freezing and canning, modern-day Japanese still eat many foods only in their appointed season. The distinct climate changes of each season support this tradition. In winter when it is snowing and freezing winds are blowing, families enjoy sitting around a steaming pot and downing *sukiyaki* or *mizutaki* before it has a chance to cool. On the other hand, during the hot, humid summers, nothing sounds more inviting than *somen* noodles served over a bed of ice with a bowl of cold dipping sauce.

In the Zen custom, Japanese still place great value on retaining the essence of each ingredient. Dipping sauces, of which there are many, are light so as not to disguise natural flavors. Vegetables are never cooked to the point where they lose the intensity of color, much less their vitamin content.

During the Heian period around the ninth century when Japanese culture came into full flower and many of the arts were born, Japanese cuisine was developed into an aesthetic experience. The aristocrats devised *kaiseki ryori* (tea ceremony cooking), which outlined rules that governed the types of foods served, the seasonings, the natural shapes of foods, and even the coloring and appearance of the dishes on which they were served. Each dish was meant to capture conscious admiration. *Kaiseki ryori* is the grand cuisine of Japan today and is prepared for banquets and ceremonial dinners. It is credited with the attention given to visual appeal in everyday Japanese meals.

The care taken to select only the freshest ingredients and cook them briefly makes Japanese food one of the healthiest cuisines in the world. In fact, when health-food awareness caught on in the United States in the late sixties, advocates embraced many ancient Japanese foods as if they were newly discovered. *Tofu* and other soybean products are some of the richest sources of protein. Kelp and other seaweeds supply a wealth of minerals and iodine. Fish is rich in protein and low in cholesterol. And, of course, vegetables are an integral part of Japanese cooking. In recent years, Western flavors using oils and meat have become popular in Japan. But, on the whole, Japanese food is a light fare, while remaining both elegant and nourishing.

Beef and meat from other land animals have been available since Admiral Perry opened trade with Japan in 1850. However, because of the high cost and "exotic" taste, meats were primarily enjoyed by the more cosmopolitan, upper classes until after World War II. After the war, the Japanese took an avid interest in things American and today meat is a common part of the Japanese diet. It is primarily used in small quantities in *sukiyaki, shabu shabu* and other one-pot cooking dishes.

Some Japanese still find the idea of eating a slab of meat aberrant. Recently our parents received a call from a desperate Caucasian neighbor who had taken in a Japanese exchange student. It seems the woman had outdone herself to cook the most appetizing American dishes—steak, prime rib, pork chops. But the student politely picked at the vegetables, without touching the meat. After a week the girl had grown so thin and weak she looked as if she would pass out. When the concerned neighbor brought her to our parents' home, the girl admitted that she found the idea of having a large piece of meat on her plate so abhorrent she could not look at it, much less eat it. And she could not bring herself to tell her generous American hostess her problem. Our mother prepared some hot rice, a plate of raw fish, pickled vegetables and green tea and the student quickly revived.

It is not difficult to understand this love of seafood after you've visited Japan. Surrounded by water, Japan is an archipelago with four main islands, which together are about the size of California. A population of some 115 million people makes it the most densely populated nation in the world. With so little land for agriculture or cattle raising, the Japanese naturally turned to the abundant sea. They have cultivated the ocean, discovering every edible treasure it has to offer. Fish and other sea products are still the main food staples in Japan.

The climate and limited land mass have also restricted the types of vegetables and fruits that can be economically farmed. Japanese dishes use a lot of root vegetables— *daikon* (radish), carrots, *gobo* (burdock root), potatoes, bamboo shoots, ginger root, water chestnuts, lotus root—probably because they grow straight down, rather than sprawling out and consuming space.

Many Westerners are hesitant to tackle Japanese cooking because the unfamiliar flavors and attention to aesthetic presentation lead them to believe there is something mysterious and difficult involved. That is hardly the case. Japanese cooks are taught that good cooks learn to work with the ingredients on hand, rather than to strictly follow a recipe. As you get comfortable with the basics of Japanese cooking, you will find it is easily adaptable to whatever foods are available in your area. You can frequently substitute vegetables in season for the ones called for in a recipe. *Tempura,* for instance, can be made with one or two ingredients or a dozen. *Dashi* soup can be simply a broth with a single watercress sprig floating in the center or it can contain *tofu* (soybean curd), parsley and any number of items.

The Japanese are famous for adapting foreign things to their own particular taste and needs—and food is no exception. *Teppan yaki,* beef steak grilled with butter, is a recent innovation that reflects Western influence.

This book is written by two Japanese-American women, born and raised in California. Where possible, we have suggested substitutions or variations in the recipes to make them more easily adaptable to the Western kitchen. We also decided to organize the book according to courses familiar to Western cooks—soup, salad, meat, etc.—rather than by method of cooking—boiled, broiled, fried, etc.—the way Japanese cookbooks are most often arranged.

We hope you will enjoy cooking Japanese food and will make it part of your regular diet.

THE INFLUENCE OF ZEN BUDDHISM IN JAPANESE COOKING

To understand Japanese food preparation and diet, you must look to Zen Buddhist teaching, which has heavily influenced Japanese cuisine. For centuries, Zen Buddhism and Japan's limited arable land conspired to keep the Japanese diet basically vegetarian. While today seafood is an important part of Japanese food, Zen principles continue to play an integral role in cooking habits.

The Zen monks view vegetarian cooking as a method of ascetic training for the minds of those who prepare and partake of the food. They teach that you must not tamper with nature. Part of Zen discipline is to seek out the freshest and ripest ingredient and to prepare it so that it retains the essence of its taste and the intensity of its natural color.

The Buddhists emphasize five methods of food preparation, five colors and five flavors. The reference to five is to focus on five spiritual root organs—faith, energy, memory, meditation and wisdom. Even modern-day Japanese are superstitious about even numbers because they can be divided. Dinner sets, for example, are sold in odd numbers.

The five food preparation methods are uncooked, boiled, broiled, fried and steamed, and formal banquets include at least one dish from each. The five colors are green, yellow, red, white and black (or purple). And the five flavors are soy sauce, salt, sugar, vinegar and hot spices, such as mustard, ginger root and *wasabi* (horseradish). Utilizing these methods, colors and flavors, cooks must prepare dishes that are visually appealing, suitable for the season and pleasing to the palate. One reason Japanese cooks present each food in separate dishes is to preserve essential flavors.

Although Japanese cooking has come under many influences over the centuries, the Zen precepts remain very visible in the cuisine today.

NEW YEAR'S FOODS

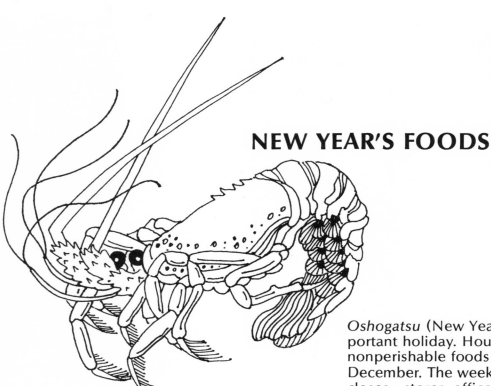

Oshogatsu (New Year's) is Japan's most important holiday. Housewives begin cooking nonperishable foods for the festivities in mid-December. The week of *Oshogatsu* everything closes—stores, offices, schools—and families reunite at their ancestral homes.

Oshogatsu is a time of tradition and superstition. Doorways of homes are decorated with bamboo, pine and *ume* plum blossoms, each with its own significance. Bamboo symbolizes strength and gentleness because it is strong yet flexible. Pine, which is forever green, represents health and longevity. And *ume* plum blossoms, which bloom around New Year's when snow is still on the ground, symbolize fidelity in the midst of adversity.

No New Year's feast is complete without *mochi* (sweet-rice cakes), which stand for both longevity and wealth (from the word *motsu* meaning "to have"). Our family gathers each year, as our ancestors had done, for *mochi-tsuki* (rice pounding). Using wooden mallets, the men pound the steaming hot rice to a fine, sticky paste and the women shape the batter into tiny round cakes.

The *mochi* is used as an ingredient in *ozoni* (see page 30), a soup that is the first meal of the year. Toasts are made with *otoso, mirin* (sweet rice wine) mixed with powdered medicinal herbs that are reputed to prevent sickness. Later the family sits down for an elaborate, beautifully presented dinner, with each dish selected for its symbolic meaning. Many of these foods are eaten year round, but at *Oshogatsu,* the cook decorates them with care. Here are some traditional New Year's foods and their meaning.

● Root vegetables, such as *daikon* (Japanese radish), *gobo* (burdock root) and carrots, are firmly planted in the soil, thus eating them at *Oshogatsu* means the family roots are deeply set, too.

● *Kombu* (dried kelp) is part of the word *yorokobu,* meaning "joy."

● *Gomame,* dried small fish, incorporates the word *mame,* meaning "health."

● *Renkon* (lotus root), cut in round slices, symbolizes the Buddhist wheel of life.

● *Dai dai,* a Japanese orange, also means "generation to generation."

● *Kuromame,* black beans with chestnuts and kelp, covers many symbols. *Mame* stands for health, *kuri* (chestnut) represents mastery or success, and *kombu* (kelp) means joy.

● Lobsters are red, a festive color, and they have long feelers that reach out into the future. *Ise-ebi,* the word for lobster, is made of the two characters meaning "sea old," because a lobster has a bent body like an old man. This signifies longevity.

● *Kaki* (persimmon) are for health and success.

● *Kazunoko* (herring roe), meaning "many children," is, of course, for fertility.

● Carp, a red fish, is eaten for its indomitable spirit. And *tai* (sea bream), which is also red, is part of the word *omedetai,* meaning "happiness." On festive occasions, fish should be served whole because there is superstition surrounding things that are "broken."

As you can see, New Year's food is imbued with meaning. Many of the traditional foods are selected because they are red or white in color, red symbolizing happiness and white standing for honesty and purity.

In Japan, traditional people usually taper off the celebration by eating *okayu* (soft cooked rice) prepared with seven types of green leaves on the seventh day of the new year. On the fifteenth day, they close the celebration by eating red beans with *okayu.*

We have included many New Year's foods in this book, but since they are also part of the day-to-day cooking, we did not feature them separately.

ESSENTIAL KITCHEN UTENSILS

LONG COOKING CHOPSTICKS (*hashi*) Available in bamboo or wood in various lengths, beginning at about one foot. Usually joined at one end by a small piece of string, which can be removed if desired.

GRATERS (*oroshigane*) Japanese graters are made with small sharp spikes and grate much finer than Western ones. *Oroshigame* are used to turn *daikon* (Japanese radish), ginger root and *wasabi* (Japanese horseradish powder) into a smooth mush. Today they are made in stainless steel, aluminum and plastic. A multipurpose Western grater can be used for shredding vegetables.

STEAMER (*seiro*) Usually square in shape and made of aluminum. A large bottom vessel holds boiling water, and a set of grates or tiers on which foods are set stands above. The steam from the boiling water circulates up through the tiers to cook the foods. Round, Chinese-style bamboo steamers (*mushiki*) are also commonly used.

MORTAR (*suribachi*) Available in various sizes, ranging from about five inches to one foot across. A nine-inch one is suitable for home use. Traditionally made of pottery, the bowl has a fine-textured pattern that facilitates the grinding process. Today, mortars can be found in molded plastic, though these are not recommended. A wooden pestle (*surikogi*) comes with the mortar.

SIEVES An ordinary wire-mesh Western sieve is used for draining and sieving foods. A small sieve is handy for introducing *miso* into simmering stock.

FISH KNIFE (*sashimi-bocho*) Thin-bladed, long knife for cutting fish fillets. The best ones are made of carbon steel. Blunt-tipped ones are favored in Tokyo, while pointed ones are popular in Osaka.

VEGETABLE KNIFE (*nakiri-bocho*) Broad-bladed knife for paring, slicing, chopping and mincing vegetables. Tokyo cooks prefer the rounded-end style, while Osaka cooks use blunt-end ones. Ideally made of high-quality carbon steel.

RICE PADDLE (*shamoji*) A wooden paddle-shaped utensil used for serving rice.

BAMBOO SUSHI MAT (*maki-su*) Strips of bamboo woven into a mat and secured with string. Commonly about ten inches square and used principally for rolling *sushi*. The width of the strips vary from thick to thin, the former used for making thin-rolled *sushi*, the latter (an *onizu*) for thicker rolls, such as *tamago yaki* (sweet egg roll).

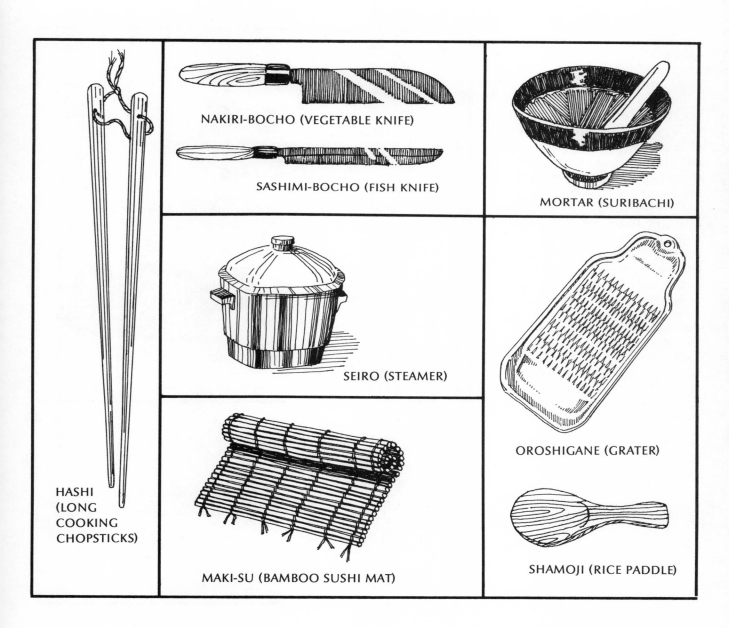

HASHI
(LONG
COOKING
CHOPSTICKS)

NAKIRI-BOCHO (VEGETABLE KNIFE)

SASHIMI-BOCHO (FISH KNIFE)

MORTAR (SURIBACHI)

SEIRO (STEAMER)

OROSHIGANE (GRATER)

MAKI-SU (BAMBOO SUSHI MAT)

SHAMOJI (RICE PADDLE)

RICE COOKER An electric appliance that makes perfect rice every time. (See page 105.)

RECTANGULAR EGG PAN *(tamago yaki nabe)* Commonly available in cast iron or heavyweight aluminum, though the best ones (and most expensive) are made of copper coated with tin. Do not scrub with abrasive material; after use, wipe it out with some oil and a clean cloth. Season the pan before initial use by cooking some vegetables in a couple of tablespoons of oil.

TEMPURA WIRE LADLE A mesh scoop with long handle used for retrieving cooked *tempura* (though this can be done with cooking chopsticks) and for removing loose batter from the oil.

RICE COOKER

TAMAGO YAKI NABE (RECTANGULAR EGG PAN)

TEMPURA WIRE LADLE

PLACE SETTING AND SERVING DISHES

LONG DISH

PLACE SETTING

STEAMED EGG CUSTARD CUP

DIPPING SAUCE CUP

NOODLE BASKET

DONBURI BOWL

CONDIMENT DISH

DIPPING BOWL

TEA POT AND CUP

CUTTING TECHNIQUES AND DECORATIVE CUTS

To make a fan form for garnish, make lengthwise narrow cuts through radish to within about 1/4 inch of the base. Then "fan" open.

To achieve this chrysanthemum cut, place radish between two chopsticks and cut vertically and horizontally.

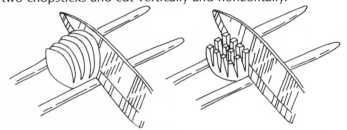

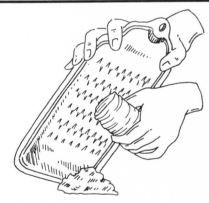

For cutting vegetables into matchstick size, first cut into thin slabs, then stack the slabs and cut lengthwise into long, thin strips.

In simmered foods, cut *gobo* (burdock root), carrots or bamboo shoots diagonally, making a quarter turn with each cut.

Slice cucumber thinly at diagonal slant for *sunomono* (vinegared foods) to allow better absorption of dressing.

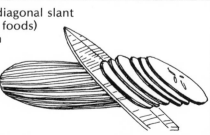

To grate *daikon* (Japanese radish), move the vegetable across pointed spikes of the grater in quick, even strokes.

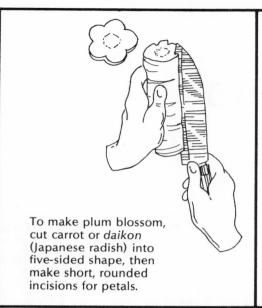

To make plum blossom, cut carrot or *daikon* (Japanese radish) into five-sided shape, then make short, rounded incisions for petals.

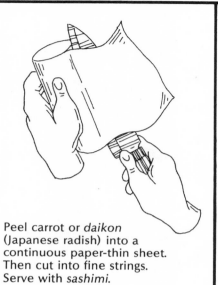

Peel carrot or *daikon* (Japanese radish) into a continuous paper-thin sheet. Then cut into fine strings. Serve with *sashimi*.

For *chirashizushi* (vegetable *sushi* rice), shave carrots and *gobo* (burdock root) much like you would whittle a stick.

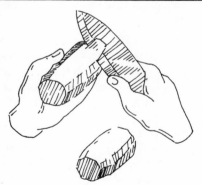

For simmered dishes, cut end off *sato imo* (taro potato) or turnip, then peel to get flat eight- or five-sided shape.

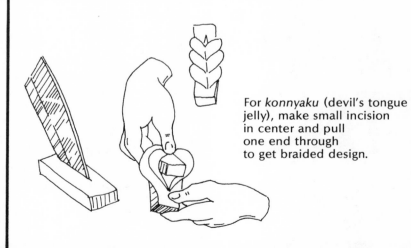

For *konnyaku* (devil's tongue jelly), make small incision in center and pull one end through to get braided design.

Shirumono
SOUPS

DASHI
Soup Stock

Dashi is the omnipresent ingredient that gives Japanese cooking its distinct flavor. A broth made with *katsuobushi* (dried bonito shavings) and *kombu* (dried kelp), *dashi* is used as a base for soups and sauces and as stock for a variety of simmered dishes.

Dashi is a clear, mild-tasting consommé. If you find the flavor unpleasant, however, you can substitute a thin chicken stock without considerably altering the taste of a dish.

There are two types or "degrees" of *dashi. Ichiban dashi,* a clear broth, is considered the basic soup stock. *Niban dashi,* which is merely the ingredients reserved from the preparation of *ichiban dashi* reheated with additional *katsuobushi,* has a richer flavor and is favored as cooking stock.

While many cooking purists prefer to make *dashi* from scratch, it's not necessary. A number of very good, instant *dashi-no-moto* brands in teabaglike filters, granule packets and bouillonlike cubes are on the market. Most home cooks appreciate the convenience of instant *dashi.* We recommend it.

If refrigerated in a tightly sealed container, *dashi* will keep for up to two weeks.

NUMBER ONE SOUP STOCK
Ichiban Dashi

4- by 6-inch piece *dashi kombu* (dried kelp)
5 cups water
1-1/2 cups *katsuobushi* (dried bonito shavings)

Wipe *kombu* with damp cloth and make several slits along sides to bring out more flavor. Combine *kombu* and water in a pan and let stand 1 hour. Place saucepan over medium heat and bring to a boil. Immediately remove *kombu* (reserve for making *Niban Dashi,* following) and add *katsuobushi.* Boil for 45 seconds and turn off heat. Allow *katsuobushi* to settle to bottom of pan, then strain through cheesecloth or fine sieve. (Reserve *katsuobushi* for making *Niban Dashi.*)
Makes approximately 5 cups

NUMBER TWO SOUP STOCK
Niban Dashi

Leftover *kombu* and *katsuobushi* from *Ichiban Dashi* (preceding)
4 cups water
Additional 1/2 cup *katsuobushi* (dried bonito shavings)

Place leftover *kombu* and *katsuobushi* in pan with water. Bring to a boil. Remove *kombu* immediately. Add the additional 1/2 cup *katsuobushi* and boil for 3 minutes. Remove from heat. Strain through cheesecloth or fine sieve. Makes approximately 4 cups

KELP SOUP STOCK
Kombu Dashi

4- by 6-inch piece *dashi kombu* (dried kelp)
4-1/2 cups water

Wipe *kombu* with damp cloth and make several slits along sides to bring out more flavor. Combine *kombu* and water in a pan and let stand for 2 hours. Bring to a boil. Remove *kombu* immediately and skim off foam from broth.
Makes approximately 4-1/2 cups

IRIKO SOUP STOCK
Iriko Dashi

4- by 6-inch piece *dashi kombu* (dried kelp)
1/2 cup *iriko* (small dried fish), heads and innards removed
4-1/2 cups water

Wipe *kombu* with damp cloth and make several slits along sides to bring out more flavor. Place *iriko* and *kombu* in pan with water and let stand for 45 minutes. Bring to a boil over medium heat. Remove *kombu* immediately. Lower heat and cook *iriko* for 15 minutes longer. Strain broth through fine sieve or cheese-cloth.
Makes approximately 4-1/2 cups

NOTE Many people don't bother to remove the heads and innards of the *iriko* because the fish themselves are so tiny that very little is left if you remove any part. Leaving the fish intact gives the broth a slightly bitter flavor.

SUIMONO
Clear Soup

Suimono (clear soup) epitomizes the simplicity and reverence for nature so basic to Japanese cooking. Subtle and light in flavor, the pale soup is often accented with a thin lemon rind, a few *enokitake* (tiny white mushrooms), cubes of *tofu* (soybean curd), a sliced carrot shaped like a flower or a single leaf floating in the broth. Ingredients should be kept to a minimum, used only to give a flash of color. Clear soup is not meant to serve as a meal, but merely to whet the appetite.

Japanese serve soup in shiny, lacquer bowls with lids that complement the naturalness of the ingredients. When eating, it is proper to pick out the food with chopsticks and sip the broth directly from the bowl.

4-1/2 cups *dashi*
1/2 teaspoon salt
1/4 teaspoon light soy sauce
4 leaves *mitsuba* (trefoil) or parsley
Four 1/3-inch-thick slices *kamaboko* (fish cake)
4 slivers lemon rind

Bring *dashi* to a boil and add salt and soy sauce. Divide *mitsuba* and *kamaboko* among 4 individual soup bowls and pour *dashi* over. Add a thin sliver of lemon rind to each bowl for fragrance.
Makes 4 servings

VARIATIONS Practically any vegetable may be substituted for the *mitsuba* and *kamaboko*. Some favorites are sliced carrots, whole snow peas, softened and slivered *shiitake* (dried mushrooms), slivered fresh mushrooms, whole bean sprouts, julienned bell peppers, softened and chopped *wakame* (dried seaweed), cubed *tofu* (soybean curd), thinly sliced green onions, sliced okra, thinly sliced scallions, and watercress leaves. Use ingredients sparingly—simplicity is the rule.

MISO SHIRU
Miso Soup

In traditional Japanese homes, *miso shiru* (*miso* soup) is always served for breakfast. High in protein and containing lactobacillus and other digestive enzymes, this soup is considered a good way to get yourself off to an energetic start.

It is considered proper to serve *miso shiru* with any meal, however. Many an Issei grandparent has regaled his or her grandchild with stories about being so poor that all the family had to live on was "rice, *miso* soup and pickled vegetables"—not a luxurious meal, but certainly nutritious enough for subsistence.

Miso, a fermented mixture of soybeans and malted rice, comes in a variety of tastes, depending on the region of its origin. Basically, two types, both available in the United States, are predominant. *Akamiso* (red *miso*) contains less malted rice and has a stronger flavor than *shiromiso* (white *miso*). *Akamiso* is usually preferred in Kanto cooking (the region around Tokyo). *Shiromiso* is used more often in Kansai cooking (the region around Osaka and Kyoto). Kansai food is normally lighter and sweeter in taste and more colorful in presentation than Kanto, typically a heavier, heartier fare.

You can use either red or white *miso*, depending on your personal preference, or you can combine them.

MISO SOUP WITH TOFU AND WAKAME
Tofu to Wakame no Miso Shiru

4-1/2 cups *Iriko Dashi* (page 22)
3 tablespoons *akamiso* (red soybean paste)
1 tablespoon *shiromiso* (white soybean paste)
1/4 cup *wakame* (dried seaweed), softened in lukewarm water 10 minutes, drained and cut into 1-inch lengths
1/3 cake *tofu* (soybean curd), cut into 1/2-inch cubes
1 green onion, chopped

Bring stock to a boil. Combine the *akamiso* and *shiromiso* in a small sieve and dip the bottom of the sieve into the stock. Press the *miso* through the sieve so that it will dissolve without leaving lumps. Do not allow the *miso* to boil or the flavor will be destroyed. Add *wakame, tofu* and green onions. Remove from heat immediately and serve.
Makes 4 servings

VARIATION This recipe may be made using only *akamiso* or only *shiromiso,* if you don't have one or the other on hand. The *akamiso* is saltier and stronger in flavor than the *shiromiso.*

OYSTER MISO SOUP
Kaki no Miso Shiru

4-1/2 cups *dashi*
4 shucked fresh large oysters, cut in half
1/4 cup *shiromiso* or *akamiso* (white or red soybean paste)
1/4 teaspoon freshly grated ginger root
1 green onion, chopped

Bring *dashi* to a boil. Add oysters. Put *miso* in a small sieve and dip the bottom of the sieve into the *dashi.* Press the *miso* through the strainer so that it dissolves easily without leaving lumps. Do not allow the *miso* to boil or the flavor will be destroyed. Stir in ginger root and green onion. Remove from heat immediately and serve.
Makes 4 servings

FISH SOUP
Ushio Jiru

1/2 pound filleted white fish
    (rock cod, sea bass, perch),
    cut into bite-size pieces
Salt for seasoning fish
4-1/2 cups *Kombu Dashi*
    (page 21)
1-1/2 teaspoons salt
Dash of MSG (optional)
4 thin lemon wedges
4 sprigs watercress

Sprinkle the fish lightly with
salt. Bring stock to a boil. Add
fish and return to a boil.
Season with salt and MSG.
Pour into 4 individual bowls
and garnish each with a lemon
wedge and a watercress sprig.
Serve immediately.
Makes 4 servings

ABALONE SOUP
Awabi no Sumashi

1 cup liquid from canned
    abalone
3-1/2 cups water
3/4 teaspoon salt
Dash of MSG (optional)
1/3 cake *tofu*, (soybean curd),
    cut into 1/2-inch cubes
8 thin slices canned abalone
4 slivers lemon rind
2 leaves spinach, parboiled
    2 minutes, drained and cut
    into 1-inch lengths

Combine abalone liquid, water, salt and MSG and bring
to a boil. Skim off any foam.
Add *tofu* and abalone slices.
Quickly return to a boil and
immediately remove from heat.
Pour into 4 individual bowls
and garnish each with a sliver
of lemon rind and a few
strands of spinach.
Makes 4 servings

VARIATION   Egg is a good addition to this soup. After soup
returns to second boil, beat 2
eggs and slowly pour into
soup stock while stirring constantly. The eggs should form
long strands as they are stirred
into the stock.

CLAM SOUP
Kai Jiru

12 clams in the shell
2 teaspoons salt
Dash of MSG (optional)
4 thin lemon wedges
4 sprigs parsley or watercress

Soak clams in cold water to
cover for about 4 hours to
release sand. Then scrub shells
clean under cold, running water.
    Place clams in saucepan,
add cold water to cover (about
6 cups) and bring to a boil.
When the clams open, re-
move from the saucepan,
season broth with salt and
MSG and heat to boiling
point. Divide clams, lemon
wedges and parsley sprigs
evenly among 4 individual
bowls. Pour in hot broth and
serve immediately.
Makes 4 servings

SHRIMP SOUP
Ebi to Somen Shiru

5 shrimp
5 cups *dashi*
1 teaspoon salt
Dash of MSG (optional)
15 dried *somen* noodles,
  boiled in water for 3 minutes or until cooked and
  drained
5 sprigs watercress

Shell the shrimp, leaving the tails intact. Devein them, and then continue to cut in half along the vein line but not all the way through to butterfly.

Bring *dashi* to a boil, add the shrimp and boil for 2 minutes, or until shrimp turn pink. Season with salt and MSG and remove from heat.

Place 3 *somen* noodles and a sprig of watercress in each of 5 individual serving bowls. Pour in the shrimp and broth and serve immediately.
Makes 5 servings

NOTE Do not overcook the shrimp or they will become tough.

SEAWEED SOUP
Nori no Otsuyu

1/2 pound pork, cut into
    strips
1 clove garlic, minced
    (optional)
Vegetable oil, if needed
5-1/2 cups water
3 fresh or canned water
    chestnuts, sliced into thin
    rounds
1-1/2 teaspoons salt
1/2 teaspoon soy sauce
1/8 teaspoon MSG (optional)
1 egg, beaten
4 sheets *nori* (dried laver),
    lightly toasted over very
    low heat on stove until crisp
1 green onion, finely chopped

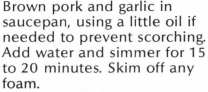

Brown pork and garlic in saucepan, using a little oil if needed to prevent scorching. Add water and simmer for 15 to 20 minutes. Skim off any foam.

Add water chestnuts, salt, soy sauce and MSG and simmer for a few minutes. Slowly pour the beaten egg into soup, stirring constantly so that the egg forms long strands. Then crumble *nori* into soup. Garnish with chopped onion before serving.

Makes 5 or 6 servings

VARIATIONS Parsley, watercress or any parboiled green vegetable may be substituted for the green onion. The egg may be omitted for a clear broth. If desired, add small cubes of *tofu* (soybean curd) to the bowls before pouring in soup.

EGG SOUP
Tamago Jiru

4-1/2 cups *dashi* or chicken stock
1-1/4 teaspoons salt
1 teaspoon soy sauce
1 teaspoon cornstarch, dissolved in 1-1/4 tablespoons water
2 eggs, beaten
4 sprigs parsley

Bring *dashi* to a boil. Add salt and soy sauce. Pour cornstarch mixture into stock, stirring constantly, and cook until slightly thickened. Slowly pour in beaten eggs, stirring constantly so that they form long strands. Boil for 1 minute, then immediately remove from heat. Pour into 4 individual bowls and garnish each with a sprig of parsley before serving.
Makes 4 servings

OVEN-COOKED WINTER MELON SOUP
Togan Shiru

1 whole, medium *togan* (winter melon)
1/2 tablespoon vegetable oil
1/2 pound pork, cut into thin strips
Salt
4 cups chicken stock
1 tablespoon soy sauce
1 teaspoon salt
Dash of MSG (optional)
6 medium *shiitake* (dried mushrooms), softened in 2 cups lukewarm water, drained (reserve water) and quartered
6 fresh or canned water chestnuts, sliced in 1/4-inch-thick rounds
1/2 pound shrimp, shelled and deveined
4 sheets *nori* (dried laver), lightly toasted over very low heat on stove until crisp
1/2 teaspoon Oriental-style sesame-seed oil
1 green onion, finely chopped

Cut off top one third of winter melon and discard. Scoop out seeds and membrane of melon and discard. Set melon upright in deep roasting pan.

Heat vegetable oil in saucepan and stir-fry pork until cooked. Sprinkle lightly with salt. Add the chicken stock and reserved *shiitake* water and bring to a boil. Mix in the soy sauce, salt and MSG, then add the *shiitake,* water chestnuts and shrimp.

Pour broth mixture into hollow of winter melon. Bake melon at 350 degrees for 1 hour, or until the white meat of melon becomes clear.

Before serving, crumble in the *nori,* and add sesame-seed oil and green onion.

Place melon on platter to serve. Ladle the broth into individual bowls, then scoop out some of the soft melon meat to add to each serving.
Makes 6 servings

STEAMED EGG CUSTARD
Chawan Mushi

2-1/2 cups *dashi*
1/2 teaspoon salt
1 teaspoon *mirin* (sweet rice wine)
1 teaspoon soy sauce
3 eggs, lightly beaten without forming foam
4 slices *kamaboko* (fish cake)
4 slices chicken, each about the size of a shrimp
12 ginkgo nuts, parboiled and skinned (page 54)
2 leaves spinach or *mitsuba* (trefoil), cut into 1-1/2-inch lengths
4 shrimp, shelled with tails intact, deveined and lightly sprinkled with salt and *sake* (rice wine)
1 large *shiitake* (dried mushroom), softened in lukewarm water, drained and quartered

Mix together *dashi,* salt, *mirin* and soy sauce in a saucepan. Bring to a boil, remove from heat and let cool. Mix eggs with cooled soup stock. Pour egg mixture through fine strainer to ensure a smooth custard.

Divide *kamaboko,* chicken and ginkgo nuts among 4 individual serving bowls. Divide egg mixture evenly among bowls. Remove any foam on surface with a spoon. Place an equal portion of spinach, shrimp and *shiitake* on top of each bowl.

Bring water in steaming unit to a boil. When water is boiling hard, place bowls in steamer. If steamer is metal, wrap the cover with a dish towel to prevent water that forms on lid from dripping into custard. Steam for 3 minutes on high heat, then reduce to medium heat and steam for 15 minutes.

Custard is done when toothpick inserted into its center comes forth clean. Serve immediately.
Makes 4 servings

MOCHI SOUP
Ozoni

5 cups *Ichiban Dashi* (page 21)
3/4 teaspoon salt
1 teaspoon soy sauce
4 to 8 *mochi* (small, plain rice cakes)
Four 1/4-inch-thick slices *kamaboko* (fish cake)
4 shrimp, shelled with tails intact, deveined, boiled 3 minutes and drained
8 leaves nappa cabbage or spinach, parboiled 2 minutes, drained and cut into 2-inch lengths

Combine the *dashi,* salt and soy sauce in a saucepan and bring to a boil.

To prepare the *mochi,* place in a small saucepan of simmering water for 1 minute or until soft, being careful not to melt them. Remove and place in 4 individual bowls. Attractively arrange the *kamaboko* slices, shrimp and cabbage leaves with the *mochi,* and pour the hot *dashi* over the arrangement.
Makes 4 servings

VARIATIONS Clams in the shell, *mitsuba* leaves (trefoil), softened and slivered *shiitake* (dried mushrooms), whole snow peas, sliced water chestnuts, sliced bamboo shoots or watercress leaves may be added. Be sure to boil them quickly in the *dashi* before pouring into serving bowls.

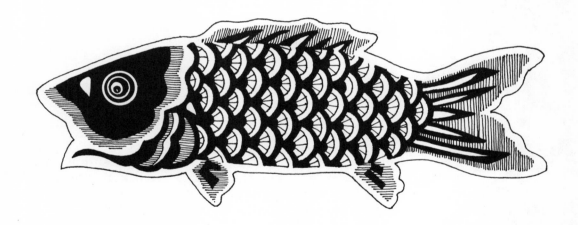

Yasai
VEGETABLES

There's no such dish as salad in Japanese cuisine because nearly every dish contains vegetables. Japanese restaurants in the United States cater to American serving customs by making *sunomono* a second course after soup. *Sunomono,* which translates as "things of vinegar," can be made with almost any raw or parboiled vegetable. Often times baby clams, shrimp, crab meat or chicken is mixed in for variety.

The Japanese use a mild rice vinegar. If none is available in your area, substitute white distilled vinegar.

The main point to remember when cooking vegetables is that they should not be overcooked. It is important that they retain their natural color, flavor and vitamin content.

DAIKON AND CARROT SALAD
Daikon Namasu

1 medium *daikon* (Japanese radish)
1 carrot
1 teaspoon salt
Toasted white sesame seeds for garnish (optional)

DRESSING
3 tablespoons Japanese rice vinegar
1-1/2 tablespoons sugar
1 tablespoon soy sauce
1 teaspoon salt
1 tablespoon *dashi*

Peel the *daikon* and cut into 2-inch lengths. Cut again lengthwise into 1/3-inch-thick strips, then cut each slice into very thin julienne strips. Peel the carrot and cut in the same way. Place *daikon* and carrot in a bowl, sprinkle with the salt and knead a little until limp. Put a heavy plate over them to weight them down and let stand for about 30 minutes.

Place the *daikon* and carrot in cold water for a few seconds, remove and squeeze out the excess water. Combine all of the dressing ingredients, stirring well to dissolve the sugar and salt, and pour the dressing over the *daikon* and carrot. Mix well. Sprinkle on sesame seeds for garnish, if desired.
Makes 4 servings

NOTE   If using white distilled vinegar, increase the sugar to 2 tablespoons.

GREEN BEAN AND GINGER SALAD
Ingen no Aemono

1 pound green beans
2 tablespoons salt
1 teaspoon white sesame
  seeds, toasted, for garnish

DRESSING
2 teaspoons *mirin* (sweet
  rice wine)
1/2 teaspoon salt
1/4 teaspoon freshly grated
  ginger root
1 tablespoon *sake* (rice wine)
3 tablespoons soy sauce
Dash of MSG (optional)

String the beans, rinse them with cold water and then rub them with the salt. Place beans in boiling water and cook until tender, about 5 minutes. Drain and rinse with cold water immediately. Allow beans to drain thoroughly, then cut into 2-inch lengths.

To dress the beans, sprinkle with the *mirin* and salt. Combine the ginger, *sake,* soy sauce and MSG and pour the mixture over the beans. Mix together thoroughly. Sprinkle on sesame seeds for garnish. Makes 4 servings

SHOGA (GINGER ROOT)

CRAB AND CUCUMBER SALAD
Kani to Kyuri Namasu

6 ounces fresh or canned
  crab meat
2 tablespoons Japanese rice
  vinegar or fresh lemon juice
1 large cucumber
1 tablespoon salt
1/8 teaspoon freshly shredded
  ginger root (optional)

DRESSING
1 tablespoon *mirin* (sweet rice
  wine)
1 teaspoon salt
3 tablespoons Japanese rice
  vinegar
1 teaspoon soy sauce

If the crab meat is in chunks, gently break it up a little with a fork, removing any shell fragments. Sprinkle 1 tablespoon of the vinegar over the crab meat and set aside.

Cut the cucumber in half lengthwise, remove the seeds and slice thinly crosswise. Sprinkle salt over the cucumber, set aside for about 5 minutes, and then gently knead in the salt until cucumber is limp. Rinse with cold water and squeeze out any excess water. Sprinkle the remaining 1 tablespoon vinegar on the cucumber and again squeeze out any excess water.

Combine all of the dressing ingredients, stirring well to dissolve the salt. Toss together the crab meat and cucumber, pour the dressing over them and mix thoroughly. Garnish with ginger. Makes 4 servings

CUCUMBER AND SEAWEED SALAD
Kyuri to Wakame Sunomono

1/4 cup *shirasuboshi* (small
  dried white fish)
3 tablespoons distilled white
  vinegar
1-1/2 tablespoons sugar
1 teaspoon soy sauce
1 teaspoon salt

1/2 teaspoon salt
2 cucumbers, very thinly sliced
1 tablespoon distilled white
  vinegar

1/2 cup *wakame* (dried
  seaweed)
1 tablespoon distilled white
  vinegar

Finely slivered *shiso* (green
  beefsteak leaves) or ginger
  root for garnish (optional)

Rinse the dried fish in cold,
running water, drain well and
soak them in the vinegar,
sugar, soy sauce and salt for
5 to 10 minutes.

Gently knead the salt into
the sliced cucumbers, rinse
with cold water and squeeze
out the excess water. Sprinkle
the vinegar onto the cucumbers, and squeeze out the
water once again.

Pour hot water over the
wakame and let stand until it
softens. Drain and cut into
bite-size strips. Mix in the
vinegar.

Combine the fish, cucum-
bers and *wakame,* including
the mixture the fish was soaking in, and mix well. Garnish
with slivered *shiso,* if desired.
Makes 4 servings

VARIATIONS Substitute well
drained, canned baby clams,
bay shrimp or flaked crab
meat for the *shirasuboshi,*
but do not rinse with water.
Proceed as directed.

RAINBOW SALAD
Nana Iro Namasu

2 ounces dried *shirataki* (yam
  noodles)
4 tablespoons Japanese rice
  vinegar
1 small *daikon* (Japanese
  radish)
1 small carrot, peeled
1 cucumber, halved and
  deseeded
Salt
1 large pom-pom chrysanthemum, preferably yellow
1 tomato
1/2 block *kamaboko* (red fish
  cake)

DRESSING
2 tablespoons sugar
2/3 teaspoon salt
2 tablespoons Japanese rice
  vinegar
Juice of 1/2 lemon
1/4 cup white sesame seeds,
  toasted and crushed

Boil the *shirataki* in water until tender, drain and pour cold water over to cool. Squeeze out excess water, cut into 1-1/2- to 2-inch lengths and place in a bowl. Sprinkle on 1 tablespoon of vinegar, and set aside.

Cut the *daikon,* carrot and cucumber into julienne strips. Knead in a little salt, rinse with cold water and squeeze out the water. Sprinkle with 2 tablespoons of the vinegar and squeeze out liquid again.

Wash the chrysanthemum and pull off petals. Add the remaining tablespoon vinegar to a pot of boiling water, and drop the petals in for a few seconds. Drain and then immerse petals in cold water to arrest cooking. Drain well.

Cut the tomato in half and discard the seeds. Cut into strips. Cut the *kamaboko* lengthwise into 3 pieces and then cut crosswise into 1/4-inch-wide strips.

Mix all of the dressing in-gredients together, stirring well to dissolve the sugar and salt, and combine with the vegetables, chrysanthemum petals and *kamaboko.* Mix well and chill before serving. Makes 6 servings

VARIATION   Substitute 1 block *konnyaku* (devil's tongue jelly), cut in matchstick-size pieces, for the *shirataki.* Omit boiling. Sprinkle with vinegar as directed for *shirataki* and proceed as directed.

EGGPLANT AND SOYBEAN SALAD
Nasu to Edamame Goma-ae

4 to 6 Japanese eggplants
1 teaspoon *yakimyoban* (Japanese alum)
1/2 cup fresh soybeans
4 *shiso* (green beefsteak leaves), thinly sliced, for garnish (optional)

DRESSING
3 tablespoons white sesame seeds, toasted
1/4 teaspoon salt
1-1/2 tablespoons soy sauce
1-1/2 tablespoons *dashi*

Wash the eggplants, cut in half lengthwise and then slice 1/8 inch thick. Soak the eggplants in water to cover and *yakimyoban* for about 5 to 10 minutes. Drain and boil in clean water for 4 minutes. Drain and squeeze out the excess water. Boil the soybeans in their pods for 10 minutes. Drain, cool and remove and discard the pods.

Mix together all of the dressing ingredients and combine with the eggplants and soybeans. Garnish with the *shiso,* if desired. Serve at room temperature or chilled. Makes 4 servings

ASPARAGUS AND MISO SAUCE
Asuparagasu to Sumiso

1 pound asparagus
2 teaspoons salt

SAUCE
1/2 cup *shiromiso* (white soybean paste)
2 tablespoons Japanese rice vinegar
1-1/2 tablespoons sugar
1 tablespoon *mirin* (sweet rice wine)
1 teaspoon freshly grated ginger root (optional)
Dash of MSG (optional)

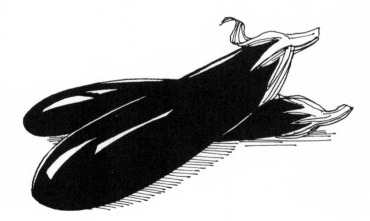

Break off tough ends of asparagus and wash spears. Bring a generous amount of water and the salt to a boil and add the asparagus. Return to a boil, then turn off heat. Cover and let stand for 10 minutes. Drain and run cold water over asparagus to retain bright color.

Mix together all of the sauce ingredients to make a soft paste. Serve in a little dish as a dipping sauce for asparagus or cut asparagus into 1-1/2-inch lengths, pour sauce over, toss and serve as a salad.
Makes 4 servings

EGGPLANTS WITH MISO
Nasu no Dengaku

4 medium Japanese eggplants
1/2 cup *shiromiso* (white soybean paste)
2 tablespoons *sake* (rice wine)
2 tablespoons *mirin* (sweet rice wine)
2 tablespoons sugar
3 tablespoons vegetable oil
3 tablespoons white sesame seeds, toasted

Wash the eggplants; remove the sepals but leave the stems on. Cut the eggplants in half lengthwise. If necessary, slice off the center of the skin side so that the eggplant halves will stand flat. Make 2 or 3 diagonal slits across the flesh side of the eggplant halves.

Mix together the *miso, sake, mirin* and sugar and set aside.

In a skillet, heat the oil over medium heat. Fry the eggplants flesh side down until light brown. Turn over and fry the skin side until the eggplants are done. Spread the *miso* mixture on top of the eggplants and sprinkle with the sesame seeds. Broil the eggplants just long enough to heat the *miso*. Serve immediately.
Makes 4 servings

NOTE   This dish may also be made with *akamiso* (red soybean paste). If using this type of *miso*, increase sugar measure to 1/4 cup.

BEAN SPROUT SALAD
Moyashi Sunomono

1 pound fresh bean sprouts
2 tablespoons Japanese rice
   vinegar
3 tablespoons soy sauce
1 tablespoon Oriental-style
   sesame-seed oil
1/2 teaspoon sugar
1 tablespoon white sesame
   seeds, toasted and ground
2 thin slices ginger root,
   minced, or
   1 teaspoon slivered *beni
   shoga* (pickled ginger)
1 bunch watercress, washed
   and stemmed

Clean bean sprouts, removing brown root part, and wash in cold water. Parboil for 1 minute and drain. Rinse under cold water and drain well. Sprinkle with 1 tablespoon of the vinegar. Mix together the remaining 1 tablespoon vinegar, the soy sauce, sesame-seed oil, sugar, sesame seeds and ginger and pour over bean sprouts and watercress. Toss well. Chill before serving.
Makes 4 servings

CUCUMBER AND NOODLE SALAD
Harusame Kyuri Namasu

3 ounces dried *harusame*
   (thin, transparent noodles)
1/2 teaspoon salt
2 small or 1 large cucumber,
   thinly sliced
1/2 block *kamaboko* (fish
   cake), cut crosswise into
   1/4-inch-thick slices, then
   slices cut into 1/4-inch-
   wide strips

DRESSING
2 tablespoons sugar
1 teaspoon salt
3 tablespoons fresh lemon
   juice
3 tablespoons Japanese rice
   vinegar
Dash of MSG (optional)

Boil the *harusame* in salted water for 7 minutes. Drain in colander and rinse with cold water. Drain again and cut into 1-1/2-inch-long pieces. Lightly salt the cucumbers and gently knead until limp. Gently squeeze out excess water with hands.

Place cucumbers in bowl with *harusame* and *kamaboko*. Mix together all of the dressing ingredients, pour over the vegetables and toss well.
Makes 4 servings

BROCCOLI SALAD WITH MUSTARD SAUCE
Broccoli no Karashi-ae

1 bunch broccoli
2 to 3 tablespoons *mirin* (sweet rice wine)
1/8 teaspoon MSG (optional)
1-1/2 teaspoons dry mustard, mixed with 1-1/2 teaspoons hot water
2 tablespoons soy sauce
2 tablespoons *dashi*

Wash the broccoli, trim off tough ends and cut into bite-size pieces. Cook in boiling salted water for about 3 minutes, or until desired tenderness. Drain, but do not rinse with cold water. Sprinkle on the *mirin* and MSG and cool the broccoli by fanning. Mix together the mustard, soy sauce and *dashi,* and pour it over the cooled broccoli, tossing it gently to coat.
Makes 4 servings

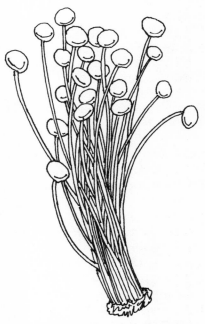

ENOKITAKE MUSHROOMS

STEAMED CHICKEN AND BEAN SPROUT SALAD
Moyashi to Tori Aemono

1 chicken breast
2 tablespoons *sake* (rice wine)
1/2 teaspoon salt
1 pound fresh bean sprouts, parboiled 1 minute, drained and cooled
1 stalk celery, thinly sliced
White sesame seeds for garnish (optional)

DRESSING
1/4 cup *dashi* or chicken stock
1 tablespoon Japanese rice vinegar
1 tablespoon sugar
1 teaspoon *shiromiso* (white soybean paste)
1 tablespoon peanut butter
1/2 teaspoon Oriental-style sesame-seed oil
1/2 teaspoon salt
2 tablespoons soy sauce

Sprinkle the chicken breast with the *sake* and salt and steam over gently boiling water for about 15 minutes, or until done. Let cool, bone and skin the chicken breast. Shred the meat and place it in the juice collected in the steamer plate.

Combine the chicken and its juice with the bean sprouts and celery. Thoroughly mix together all of the dressing ingredients, and pour over the chicken and vegetables. Sprinkle on sesame seeds for garnish, if desired.
Makes 4 servings

CHICKEN AND BEAN SPROUT SALAD
Tori to Moyashi no Sumiso-ae

1 recipe *Shiro Karashisumiso* (page 54)
1 chicken breast, boiled until tender, boned, skinned and coarsely shredded
2 tablespoons *sake* (rice wine)
1/2 pound fresh bean sprouts, parboiled 1 minute, drained and cooled
5 or 6 pieces *myoga* (a type of Japanese ginger), slivered (optional)

Prepare the dressing and set aside. While the chicken meat is still warm, sprinkle it with the *sake* and set aside to cool. Combine the chicken, bean sprouts and *myoga* with the dressing. Mix together well and serve at room temperature.
Makes 4 servings

GREEN ONIONS AND BABY CLAMS
Nuta

1 recipe *Aka Karashisumiso*
(page 54)
1/2 cup drained canned baby
clams
1 tablespoon Japanese rice
vinegar
4 cups water
1-1/2 tablespoons salt
2 bunches green onions

Prepare the dressing and set aside. Mix the baby clams and vinegar together and set aside.

Bring the water to a boil and add the salt. Parboil onions until they turn a bright green color, then cool immediately under cold, running water. Squeeze out excess water and cut into 1-1/2-inch lengths. Combine onions and clams (reserve a few for garnish) with dressing, and mix well. Garnish with clams before serving.

Makes 4 servings

VARIATIONS   If you prefer a milder taste, use *Shiro Karashisumiso* (page 54).

Substitute chopped boiled squid tentacles or octopus for the clams.

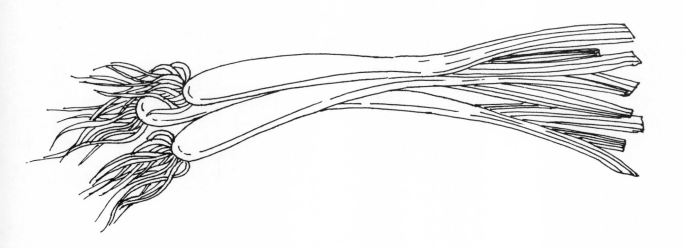

MINCED LAMB SALAD
Lamb no Lettuce Maki

4 *shiitake* (dried mushrooms)
3 green onions
1 tablespoon vegetable oil
1 teaspoon minced ginger
   root
1 clove garlic, grated
1/2 pound lamb, minced
2 tablespoons *katakuriko*
   (potato starch) or cornstarch,
   mixed with 3 tablespoons
   water
1 cup shelled green peas,
   parboiled 2 minutes and
   drained
1 head butter or romaine
   lettuce, washed and separated into leaves

SEASONINGS
2 tablespoons soy sauce
2 tablespoons *sake* (rice wine)
1/2 teaspoon sugar
1/4 teaspoon salt

SHIITAKE MUSHROOMS

Soften the *shiitake* in luke-warm water; drain, reserving enough of the soaking water to measure 1 cup; set aside. Cut the green onions and *shiitake* into pieces the same size as the green peas and set aside. Mix together all of the seasonings and set aside.

Heat the oil in a skillet or wok and stir-fry the ginger and garlic 10 seconds. Add the lamb, *shiitake*, and green onions and stir-fry until the lamb is cooked. Add the seasonings and stir-fry to coat all of the ingredients in the pan. Add the *shiitake* soaking liquid and bring to a boil. Add the *katakuriko* mixture and continue to stir-fry until the pan juices thicken. Add the peas, and remove from the heat. Serve with the lettuce leaves. The diners fill the leaves with the meat mixture and eat them out of hand.
Makes 4 servings

VARIATION Minced chicken or beef may be substituted for the lamb.

JAPANESE EGGPLANTS AND FRIED BEAN CURD WITH MUSTARD
Nasu to Aburage no Nibitashi

3 medium Japanese eggplants, cut into 1/3-inch-thick slices
4 cups water
1 teaspoon salt
1 piece *aburage* (deep-fried soybean curd)
1/2 cup *dashi*
2 teaspoons sugar
2 teaspoons soy sauce
1 teaspoon dry mustard, mixed with 1 teaspoon hot water
Additional 1-1/2 tablespoons soy sauce
Dash of MSG (optional)
Thinly sliced *shiso* (green beef-steak leaves) or *myoga* (a type of Japanese ginger) for garnish

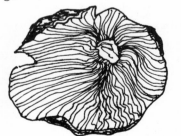

Soak the eggplant slices in water to cover for 15 minutes; drain. Bring the 4 cups of water to a boil and add the salt. Cook the eggplant in the boiling water for 2 minutes. Drain in a colander and set aside to cool. (Do not pour cold water over the eggplant.)

Pour hot water over the *aburage,* then drain and press out as much liquid as possible. Cut the *aburage* in half length-wise, and then cut crosswise into 1/3-inch-thick slices. Combine the *dashi,* sugar and 2 teaspoons soy sauce in a saucepan, add the *aburage* and cook over medium heat until most of the liquid is absorbed. Remove the *aburage* from the pan and press out any excess liquid. Combine the *aburage* and eggplant slices. Mix together the mustard, 1-1/2 tablespoons soy sauce and MSG and toss thoroughly wih the eggplants and *aburage*. Garnish with the *shiso*.
Makes 4 servings

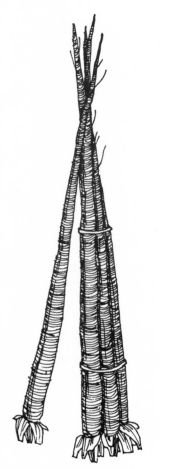

GOBO (BURDOCK ROOT)

BUTTERBUR IN SOY SAUCE DRESSING
Fuki no Aemono

5 or 6 *fuki* (butterbur)
Salt
Katsuobushi (dried bonito
   shavings) for garnish

SAUCE
1/4 cup *dashi*
2 teaspoons soy sauce
1-1/2 teaspoons salt

Sprinkle *fuki* stems lightly with salt and roll them on cutting board. The salt will ensure a bright green color when cooked. Cook the *fuki* in boiling water for about 5 to 8 minutes, or until tender, then drain.
   Fuki have fibrous skin, so you must peel the outer layer. Peel skin from top to bottom and then from bottom up. If stems are tough, tap lightly with wooden pestle to break down fibers.
   Mix together *dashi,* soy sauce and salt and pour over *fuki.* Let stand for about 30 minutes. Divide *fuki* among 4 individual bowls. Garnish with *katsuobushi* before serving.
Makes 4 servings

NOTE   *Fuki* tastes best in the spring, when the shoots are young and tender.

CRACKED BURDOCK ROOT
Tataki Gobo

1/2 pound *gobo* (burdock
   root)
4 cups water
2 teaspoons Japanese rice
   vinegar

SOAKING SAUCE
4 tablespoons *dashi*
1 tablespoon soy sauce
1 teaspoon sugar
1 teaspoon Japanese rice
   vinegar

DRESSING
2 tablespoons black sesame
   seeds, toasted
2 teaspoons Japanese rice
   vinegar
1 tablespoon soy sauce
2 teaspoons sugar

Select slim, young *gobo,* if possible. Scrub them with a vegetable brush until the brown layer of skin comes off (or scrape them with a dull knife). If *gobo* are larger than 1/2 inch in diameter, cut them in half lengthwise. As you finish preparing each *gobo,* put it in water so that it won't discolor. Drain and boil them in the 4 cups of water and the vinegar until soft, about 15 minutes; drain again. With a wooden pestle, lightly pound the *gobo* to break down the root fibers, then cut into 2-inch lengths.

Combine all of the ingredients for the soaking sauce, mix well and soak *gobo* in sauce for a few hours or overnight; drain well. Mix all of dressing ingredients in a *suribachi* (Japanese mortar). Add *gobo* and stir so that all of the pieces are completely coated with the dressing. Serve in individual dishes with all of the *gobo* pointing neatly in the same direction.
Makes 4 servings

STIR-FRIED BURDOCK ROOT
Kimpira

3 or 4 *gobo* (burdock roots), or about 4 cups cut up
1 carrot (1/2 cup cut up)
1-1/2 tablespoons Oriental-style sesame-seed or vegetable oil
2 tablespoons sugar
1/8 teaspoon *shichimi togarashi* (seven-spice mixture) or cayenne pepper (optional)
Dash of MSG (optional)
1/4 cup soy sauce
Toasted white sesame seeds for garnish

Cut the *gobo* and carrot into matchstick-like strips and soak in cold water to cover for about 20 minutes. Drain and remove excess water by wrapping in dish towel.

Heat oil in wok or heavy skillet and stir-fry *gobo* and carrot for 5 to 8 minutes over medium high heat. Add sugar, *shichimi togarashi* and MSG and mix in well. Then add soy sauce, and stir-fry until liquid is absorbed.

Sprinkle with sesame seeds before serving.
Makes 4 servings

SPINACH SHIRO-AE
Horenso no Shiro-ae

1 bunch spinach
1 block *konnyaku* (devil's
  tongue jelly), cut into
  matchstick
1/2 teaspoon instant *dashi*
  powder, mixed with
  2 tablespoons water
1 teaspoon sugar
1 tablespoon soy sauce
Dash of MSG (optional)

DRESSING
2 tablespoons white sesame
  seeds, toasted
1/2 cake *tofu* (soybean curd)
2 tablespoons *shiromiso*
  (white soybean paste)
1-1/2 tablespoons sugar
1/4 teaspoon salt
Dash of MSG (optional)

Boil the spinach in salted
water just long enough for it
to become a bright green
color. Drain and place in cold
water immediately. Drain again
and squeeze out the excess
water. Slice off and discard
the root part, then cut the
spinach into 2-inch lengths.
Set aside.

Place *konnyaku* in saucepan and cook over high heat,
stirring constantly, to remove
moisture. It is important to
remove the moisture so that
the *konnyaku* will absorb the
flavor of the sauce. When
liquid is gone, add the *dashi*,

sugar, soy sauce and MSG.
Cook until juice is nearly
evaporated.

Grind the sesame seeds in
a *suribachi* (Japanese mortar),
to an oily paste. Squeeze out
any excess water from the
tofu and push it through a
sieve. Add the *tofu* to the
sesame-seed paste, and grind
until it becomes smooth. Grind
in the *miso*, sugar, salt and
MSG until well blended. Mix
together well with the spinach
and *konnyaku*. Serve at room
temperature or chilled.
Makes 4 servings

VARIATION   In place of
konnyaku, or in addition to it,
add matchstick-cut carrots.
Parboil carrots first and proceed as directed for *konnyaku*.

SPINACH WITH SESAME SEEDS
Horenso no Goma-ae

1 pound spinach, trimmed
3 tablespoons black sesame
  seeds
2 tablespoons soy sauce
1 tablespoon sugar
Dash of MSG (optional)

Wash the spinach well and parboil for 2 minutes in lightly salted water. Drain and place in cold water immediately to retain the green color. Gently squeeze out the excess water, forming the spinach into a long, slender mass, and cut into 1-1/2-inch lengths.

Grind sesame seeds in a *suribachi* (Japanese mortar) or with a rolling pin until fine. Add sesame seeds, soy sauce, sugar and MSG to spinach, and mix together well.
Makes 4 servings

SPINACH WITH DASHI SAUCE
Horenso no Aemono

2 bunches spinach, trimmed
1/2 cup *dashi*
1/4 cup soy sauce
1-1/2 tablespoons *mirin*
  (sweet rice wine)
Katsuobushi (dried bonito
  shavings), toasted *nori*
  (dried laver) or toasted white
  sesame seeds for garnish
  (optional)

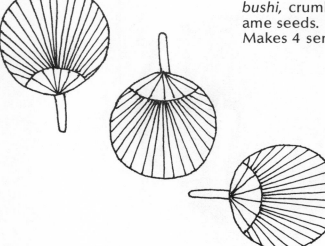

Wash the spinach well and parboil for 2 minutes in lightly salted water. Drain and place in cold water immediately to retain the green color. Gently squeeze out the excess water, forming the spinach into a long, slender mass, and then cut into four 2-inch lengths. Stand the spinach up lengthwise in 4 individual serving dishes.

Before serving, combine the *dashi*, soy sauce and *mirin* and heat in a small saucepan. Pour over the spinach portions. Garnish with *katsuobushi*, crumbled *nori* or sesame seeds.
Makes 4 servings

JAPANESE PUMPKIN
Kabocha

1 medium (3 to 4 pounds)
  kabocha (Japanese pumpkin)
1 teaspoon salt
1/2 cup *ito kombu* (string
  seaweed), softened in lukewarm water and drained
1-1/2 cups *dashi,* or as needed
1 tablespoon sugar
2 tablespoons *mirin* (sweet
  rice wine)
3 tablespoons light soy sauce

Wash the *kabocha,* cut in half and remove and discard the seeds and strings. The skin may be partially peeled or left on. Cut the *kabocha* into 1-1/2-inch cubes and rub the salt on the cubes. Add the *ito kombu* to the cubes and let stand for about 10 minutes. Transfer to a saucepan, add enough *dashi* to cover the pumpkin, and heat until the *dashi* boils. Mix in the sugar, *mirin* and soy sauce, reduce the heat and cook until the *kabocha* is tender and most of the liquid is absorbed, about 25 to 30 minutes. Serve warm or at room temperature. Makes 4 servings

KABOCHA (PUMPKIN)

BEAN CURD WHEY AND VEGETABLES
Okara no Irini

2 pieces *aburage* (deep-fried soybean curd)
1/2 carrot, cut into matchstick
4 *shiitake* (dried mushrooms), softened in 1 cup lukewarm water, drained (reserve water) and cut into matchstick
1/2 block *konnyaku* (devil's tongue jelly), cut into matchstick
1/2 cup finely slivered *gobo* (burdock root), parboiled 2 minutes and drained
3 tablespoons vegetable oil
4 to 5 cups *okara* (soybean curd whey)
1 green onion, finely chopped
1 tablespoon white sesame seeds, toasted

SEASONING
1-1/2 cups *Niban Dashi* (page 21)
1 cup water reserved from soaking *shiitake*
1/3 cup soy sauce
1/4 cup sugar
1/4 cup *sake* (rice wine)
2 to 3 tablespoons oil

Pour hot water over *aburage* to remove excess oil, then drain and cut into matchstick. Set aside with prepared carrot, *shiitake, konnyaku* and *gobo*. Mix seasoning ingredients together in a saucepan and bring to a boil. When boil starts, add the reserved ingredients. Cook for a few minutes and remove from heat.

In a wok or skillet, heat the vegetable oil. When hot, add the *okara* and stir-fry until all the oil is blended into the *okara*. Then add cooked vegetables and their juice to the *okara*. Cook over medium heat until liquid is absorbed, stirring constantly. Place in serving bowl and garnish with chopped green onion and sesame seeds. Serve hot or at room temperature.

NOTE   *Okara* is also called *kirazu* or *u no hana*. It is usually given away free at Japanese markets in California.

DEVIL'S TONGUE JELLY
Konnyaku

1/4 cup *kanjak* powder
6-3/4 cups warm water
1/2 teaspoon lye
Additional 3 to 4 quarts
  water
Salt

In a large bowl, sprinkle the *kanjak* powder into 6-1/4 cups of the warm water. Using an electric mixer (or hand beater), gradually mix together at low speed, and then beat at medium speed, scraping the sides of the bowl frequently. Beat the mixture for 6 to 7 minutes until it thickens, and then beat by hand for 10 to 15 minutes until the mixture becomes thicker and translucent. Set aside overnight.

Dissolve the lye in the remaining 1/2 cup warm water, and slowly stir the lye water into the *kanjak* mixture, being careful not to spill the lye water. Pour the mixture into a 9-by 9-inch Pyrex or stainless-steel baking pan, and smooth the surface to make a flat, even top.

Bring 3 to 4 quarts water to a boil in a stainless-steel pot. Pour a little water over the *konnyaku* before cutting to keep it from sticking back together, then cut into desired shapes and sizes. Drop pieces into the boiling water, and cook for 20 minutes after the water returns to a boil. Drain and store in a container of water in the refrigerator. The *konnyaku* will keep for about 2 weeks if the water is changed daily.

Before eating the *konnyaku*, rub it with salt and place in boiling water for 2 minutes. It is best to tear the *konnyaku* into pieces rather than cut it when using it for a recipe, if possible. Tearing it will allow the seasoning to penetrate better.
Makes one 9-inch square

DEVIL'S TONGUE JELLY WITH MISO SAUCE
Konnyaku no Misoni

2 blocks *konnyaku* (devil's
  tongue jelly)
1 tablespoon vegetable oil
1 cup *dashi*
2 tablespoons *sake* (rice
  wine)
1-1/2 tablespoons sugar
1-1/2 tablespoons *shiromiso*
  (white soybean paste)
2 teaspoons soy sauce
Dash of *shichimi togarashi*
  (seven-spice mixture)
1/4 sheet *nori* (dried laver),
  lightly toasted over very
  low heat on stove until
  crisp and cut into narrow
  1-inch-long strips, for
  garnish

Cut the *konnyaku* crosswise into 3/8-inch-thick slices. In the center of each slice, make a lengthwise 1/2-inch-long slit. Push 1 end of the slice through

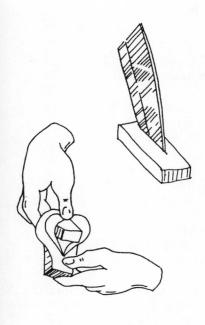

the hole and pull gently to flatten. The center will have a twisted design. Boil the *konnyaku* in water for 1 minute, then drain well.

In a skillet or wok, heat the oil. Stir-fry the *konnyaku* until liquid has evaporated. Combine the *dashi, sake* and sugar and add to the pan. Continue to stir-fry for 1 minute. Add the *miso,* and stir-fry until the liquid is absorbed. Add the soy sauce and *shichimi togarashi,* stir-fry until blended and transfer to a serving plate. Garnish with the *nori.*
Makes 4 servings

STIR-FRIED DEVIL'S TONGUE JELLY
Konnyaku no Irini

2 blocks *konnyaku* (devil's tongue jelly)
1 tablespoon vegetable oil
1 *togarashi* (dried red chili pepper), deseeded and chopped
1 tablespoon sugar
1 tablespoon *sake* (rice wine)
1-1/2 tablespoons soy sauce
Toasted white sesame seeds for garnish

Cut the *konnyaku* crosswise into 3/8-inch-thick slices. In the center of each slice, make a lengthwise 1/2-inch-long slit. Push 1 end of the slice through the hole and pull gently to flatten. The center will have a twisted design. Boil the *konnyaku* in water for 1 minute, then drain well.

In a skillet or wok, heat the oil. Add the *togarashi* and *konnyaku,* and stir-fry until liquid has evaporated. Mix together the sugar, *sake* and soy sauce, add to the pan and stir-fry until the liquid is absorbed. Garnish with sesame seeds, if desired.
Makes 4 servings

HOW TO PREPARE FRESH GINGKO NUTS

Japanese put gingko nuts in all kinds of dishes from soup and *tempura* to *sukiyaki*. Gingko nuts have a unique, nutty flavor.

Fresh gingko nuts have three outer layers that must be removed before they can be eaten. The outermost one is spongy and odiferous and has usually been removed from the nut before it is brought to market. To remove the innermost layers, crack the first one and peel it off, then boil the nuts in water for a few minutes. Drain and rub off the thin inner layer of skin. They're ready to use.

Gingko nuts can also be purchased ready to eat in cans, but the flavor and texture are far inferior to the fresh ones.

RED MISO AND MUSTARD DRESSING
Aka Karashisumiso

3 tablespoons *akamiso* (red soybean paste)
2 tablespoons sugar
1 tablespoon *sake* (rice wine)
1 teaspoon dry mustard, mixed with 1 teaspoon hot water
2 tablespoons distilled white vinegar

In a small saucepan, mix together the *miso,* sugar and *sake.* Cook over low heat for 1 minute, stirring constantly. Remove from heat and cool to room temperature. Mix in the mustard and vinegar. Makes approximately 1/3 cup

NOTE   This dressing can be used as a dip for raw vegetables. If refrigerated, it can be kept for 3 weeks or more.

WHITE MISO AND MUSTARD DRESSING
Shiro Karashisumiso

1/4 cup *shiromiso* (white soybean paste)
1 tablespoon sugar
1 tablespoon *mirin* (sweet rice wine)
2 tablespoons *dashi*
1-1/2 teaspoons dry mustard, mixed with 1-1/2 teaspoons hot water
2-1/2 tablespoons distilled white vinegar

In a small saucepan, mix together the *miso,* sugar, *mirin* and *dashi.* Cook over low heat for 1 minute, stirring constantly. Remove from heat and let cool to room temperature. Mix in the mustard and vinegar.
Makes approximately 1/2 cup

VEGETABLE DIP
Aegoromo

1 tablespoon *shiromiso*
   (white soybean paste)
2 tablespoons mayonnaise
2-1/2 tablespoons *mirin*
   (sweet rice wine)
1 tablespoon peanut butter
1 teaspoon Oriental-style
   sesame-seed oil
1 teaspoon sugar
1 tablespoon distilled white
   vinegar
Dash of MSG (optional)

Combine all of the ingredients
and mix well. Serve as a dip
for cooked green beans, asparagus, cauliflower and broccoli, or for raw celery and
carrots.
Makes approximately 1/2 cup

SHUNGIKU (EDIBLE CHRYSANTHEMUM LEAVES)

Sakana
FISH

Fish is Japan's most important source of protein. It's probably not an exaggeration to say that the Japanese know every creature in the sea. If it's edible, they've undoubtedly discovered it.

In keeping with the enthusiasm of the Japanese for fresh and natural tastes, *sashimi* (raw fish) is the most exquisite delicacy. No formal dinner is complete without it. At banquets, two or three types of *sashimi* are served.

Another custom in Japan is to serve the whole fish at formal banquets, reflecting the zealousness of the Japanese to preserve things in their natural state. The formal way to serve a fish is with head and tail intact and positioned so that the head is on the left end of the plate and the stomach is on the side closest to the diner. It's more polite not to pick randomly at the fish, but to eat it from one side and work your way across.

BROILED MISO SALMON
Sake no Miso Yaki

1-1/2 pounds salmon steaks
   (4 steaks each 3/4 inch
   thick)
1/4 cup *shiromiso* (white
   soybean paste)
1/2 teaspoon sugar
1/2 tablespoon soy sauce
Dash of MSG (optional)
1 green onion, finely chopped

Place salmon in broiler set at
400 degrees and brown for
about 7 minutes on each
side.
   Combine *miso,* sugar, soy
sauce and MSG and mix well.
Spread one eighth of the
sauce on one side of each
salmon steak. Broil sauce-
covered side up for 3 minutes
or until lightly browned. Turn
steaks over, cover second
sides with remaining sauce
and broil for 3 minutes. Garnish with chopped green
onion before serving.
Makes 4 servings

LEMON-FRIED SEA BASS
Nibe no Yakimono

1 teaspoon salt
1-1/2 pounds sea bass steaks
   (4 steaks each 3/4 inch
   thick)
1 tablespoon vegetable oil
2 tablespoons butter
8 thin slices lemon
4 wedges lemon
1 *daikon* (Japanese radish),
   grated
Soy sauce

Sprinkle salt on sea bass steaks
and let stand for about 10
minutes.
   Heat oil and butter in a
skillet. Place sea bass in the
skillet and top with lemon
slices. Fry over high heat for
1 minute. Cover, lower heat
and cook for 5 minutes or
until done. Garnish with lemon
wedges and serve with *daikon*
and soy sauce.
Makes 4 servings

VARIATION Substitute salmon,
swordfish or butterfish steaks
for the sea bass.

TERIYAKI BARRACUDA
Kamasu Teriyaki

6 tablespoons soy sauce
1/4 cup *mirin* (sweet rice
   wine)
4 barracuda steaks (1/4
   pound each)

Combine the soy sauce and
mirin, and marinate the fish
steaks in this mixture for
about 20 minutes. Remove
the fish from the marinade,
reserving the marinade, and
barbecue the fish over a charcoal fire or broil in the oven
for about 5 minutes on each
side, or until done. Handle
the fish steaks carefully so
they do not break up.
   In a small saucepan, heat
the reserved marinade until it
thickens slightly. When the
fish is cooked, brush the
steaks with the sauce for a
glossy finish.
Makes 4 servings

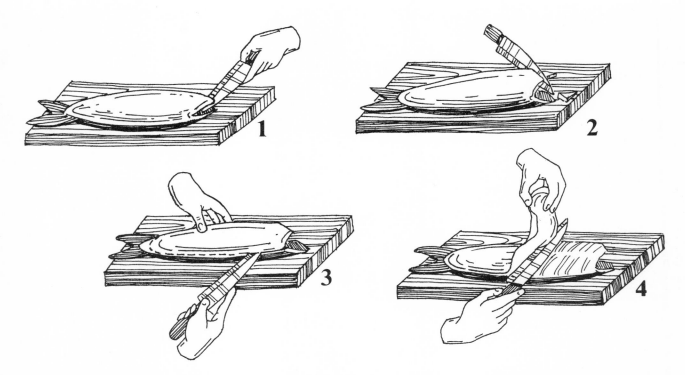

HOW TO FILLET A FISH

Filleting a fish is an art that requires considerable practice to perfect. Many of us are fortunate to have access to a market that sells fish already filleted. If, however, you find yourself in the position of having to fillet one, this brief illustrated description should be of help.

For an oval-shaped fish, such as a trout, mackerel, tuna or any fish with a thick mid-section, first lay it on a firm, flat surface and cut off the head just behind the gills. Insert a sharp, flexible-bladed knife at the point where the head was severed, making sure the blade is resting on the backbone. Cut the fish in half lengthwise by guiding the knife along the backbone to the tail end. Lift off the top half of the fish and set it aside. The backbone is now visible on the bottom half of the fish. Slide the knife blade just under the backbone at the head end and guide the knife along the bone to the tail, lifting the bone away from the flesh as you work. Remove the fins and any bony edges from the fish halves and then lay each half skin side down and carefully cut the flesh from the skin.

If you are filleting a flat fish, such as a petrale sole,

leave the head on and begin cutting along the backbone just behind it. First cut at an angle through the flesh until you reach the backbone, then slide the knife along it to the tail end and bring it up and out the top side of the fish. Set the top half aside, turn the bottom one over so that it is skin side up and repeat the procedure. Place each half skin side down and cut the flesh from the skin.

FRIED BOILED FISH
Sakana no Abura Kake

This recipe simulates the delicious taste of fried fish without the lingering odor that it often leaves. Quick to prepare, it should be made just before serving so the fish remains hot.

1-1/2 pounds red snapper fillets (4 pieces)
1/8 teaspoon MSG (optional)
1/4 cup soy sauce
2 or 3 green onions, finely chopped
3 tablespoons minced ginger root
1/3 cup vegetable oil

If fish has not been skinned, make diagonal slashes on skin side to keep it from curling.

In a shallow skillet, bring to a boil enough salted water to cover fish. Add fish and boil only until just tender, being careful not to overcook the fillets. Carefully drain fish and arrange on a serving platter. Sprinkle fillets with MSG, soy sauce, green onions and ginger.

Heat oil until *very* hot and pour over fish. (Oil should be hot enough to crackle when it touches the fish.) Serve immediately.
Makes 4 servings

VARIATION   Any lean white fish fillet may be substituted for the red snapper.

SIMMERED MACKEREL
Saba no Nitsuke

1 large mackerel, cleaned
2 tablespoons finely chopped green onion

1 tablespoon white sesame seeds
2 tablespoons Oriental-style sesame-seed oil
1 clove garlic, minced
1 tablespoon sugar
1 tablespoon *akamiso* (red soybean paste)
3 tablespoons soy sauce
Dash of cayenne pepper (optional)
2 green onions, coarsely chopped
1/2 cup *sake* (rice wine) or water

Cut the fish in half lengthwise, debone, and then cut crosswise into 2-inch-wide pieces. Mix together the finely chopped green onion, sesame seeds, sesame oil, garlic, sugar, *miso* and soy sauce. Place half of the mixture on the bottom of a skillet, lay the fish on top, skin side up, and cover with the rest of the mixture. Sprinkle on the coarsely chopped green onion, and carefully add the *sake*. Cover and cook slowly over medium heat until the fish is tender, basting occasionally with the sauce.
Makes 4 servings

SPANISH MACKEREL WITH BEEFSTEAK LEAVES
Aji no Shisoage

4 Spanish mackerel,
  skinned and filleted
2 teaspoons *mirin* (sweet
  rice wine)
2 teaspoons *sake* (rice wine)
1 teaspoon sugar
1 tablespoon *shiromiso*
  (white soybean paste)
1/2 egg white, lightly beaten
16 *shiso* (green beefsteak
  leaves)
2 tablespoons *katakuriko*
  (potato starch) or
  cornstarch
Vegetable oil for deep-frying

Grind the mackerel in a
suribachi (Japanese mortar),

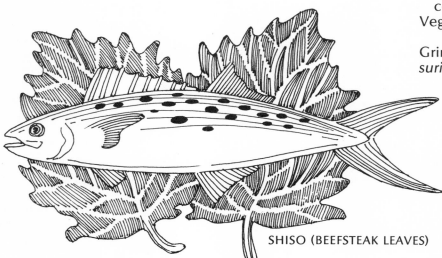

SHISO (BEEFSTEAK LEAVES)

food processor or electric blender. Add the *mirin, sake* and sugar, and continue to grind until smooth. Thoroughly mix in the *miso* and egg white.

Wash and dry the *shiso* leaves, and coat one side of each leaf with the *katakuriko*. Divide the fish mixture into 16 equal portions. Using a knife, spread the coated side of each leaf with a fish portion, and then fold the leaf in half to enclose the fish.

In a pan, heat oil to a depth of 3 inches to 375 degrees. Deep-fry the filled leaves until done, about 5 minutes. Serve hot or at room temperature.
Makes 4 servings

NOTE   If beefsteak leaves are not available, use sheets of *nori* (dried laver), cut in 2- by 3-inch pieces.

DEEP-FRIED SPANISH MACKEREL
Aji no Kara-age

8 small Spanish mackerel, cleaned
1 to 2 tablespoons salt
1 cup distilled white vinegar
1/3 cup sugar
1/3 cup light soy sauce
1 cup all-purpose flour
Vegetable oil for deep-frying
1 pound fresh bean sprouts, parboiled 1 minute and drained
1 cup grated *daikon* (Japanese radish)
4 *shiso* (beefsteak leaves) for garnish (optional)
Dash of *ichimi* (chili powder) or cayenne pepper (optional)

Lightly sprinkle the fish with salt. Mix together the vinegar, sugar and soy sauce, and set aside. Pat the fish dry with paper toweling, dredge in flour, and shake off the excess.

In a pan, heat the oil to a depth of 3 inches to about 350 degrees, and slowly deep-fry the fish, a few at a time, until just done. When all of the fish are cooked, raise the heat so that the oil is at 375 degrees, and briefly deep-fry the fish again until golden brown. Drain the fish on paper toweling, and while the fish are still hot, soak them in the vinegar mixture for 2 to 3 hours. Remove the fish from the vinegar mixture and arrange with the bean sprouts, *daikon* and *shiso* on a plate. Sprinkle a dash of cayenne pepper or chili powder over the *daikon* for more color, if desired.
Makes 4 servings

VARIATIONS Minced garlic, green onion or *togarashi* (dried red chili pepper) may be added to the vinegar mixture.

STUFFED RAINBOW TROUT
Masu no Yasai Zume

4 rainbow trout

MARINADE
2 tablespoons *sake* (rice
    wine)
2 tablespoons soy sauce

STUFFING
2/3 cup *dashi*
1 tablespoon *mirin* (sweet
    rice wine)
2 teaspoons soy sauce
1/8 teaspoon salt
1 canned bamboo shoot,
    slivered
1 small carrot, slivered
3 *shiitake* (dried mushrooms),
    softened in lukewarm
    water, drained and slivered
2 eggs, beaten

BASTING SAUCE
1 tablespoon *mirin* (sweet
    rice wine)
1 tablespoon soy sauce

Scale the trout. Cut each fish open along its back without cutting open belly side. Remove bones and innards, then rinse and dry trout.

Mix together the marinade ingredients and marinate trout for 1 hour.

To make the stuffing, combine the *dashi, mirin,* soy sauce and salt in a saucepan. Add slivered vegetables and cook over medium heat until liquid is almost completely absorbed. Stir in eggs and cook for 1 minute, stirring constantly. Remove from the heat and let cool.

Fill each trout cavity with one fourth of the stuffing, and secure cavities closed with toothpicks. Place stuffed trout in baking pan and bake in a preheated 375-degree oven for 10 minutes. Combine basting sauce ingredients and baste fish with mixture. Bake 10 minutes longer, then serve.

Makes 4 servings

SHIOYAKI
Salt Broiling

Shioyaki, which means salt broiling, is a simple technique with a surprisingly delicious result. You can prepare a number of small fish (Spanish mackerel, perch, red snapper, sea bream) this way. The one important rule is that they should always be kept whole, with skin and bones intact. The juices released from the skin and bones when broiling impart flavor to the meat. Rubbing salt into the skin of the fish serves to break down the thin layer of fat underneath. This dissolving fat makes the meat moist and tender when cooked.

Shioyaki works very well with a whole chicken, too.

SALTED RAINBOW TROUT
Masu Shioyaki

Salt
4 rainbow trout, cleaned
Soy sauce
4 wedges lemon

Evenly rub a generous amount of salt on both sides of fish and let stand about 15 minutes.

Insert a thin metal skewer near eye of each fish and weave it internally straight back toward the tail. Insert a second skewer near the mouth and weave it internally straight back toward the tail. The two skewers should be spread apart for good leverage.

Place fish on charcoal grill or in a broiler (close to heat) and cook until browned and crispy on outside. Gently turn fish over and cook until firm in center. The cooking time should total about 10 minutes, depending on size of fish. To prevent damaging skin and meat of fish, try to turn over only once.

Remove skewers and serve with soy sauce and lemon wedges.
Makes 4 servings

VARIATION Substitute any small fish—Spanish mackerel, red snapper, perch, kingfish—for the trout.

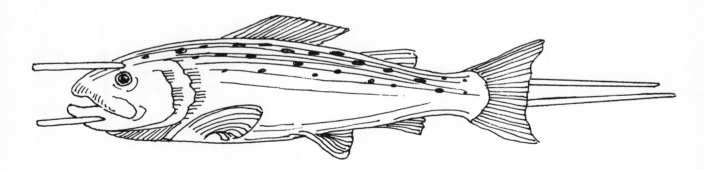

RAW OYSTERS
Sugaki

8 shucked fresh oysters
3 tablespoons distilled white
  vinegar
1 cup grated *daikon* (Japanese radish)
2 tablespoons freshly grated
  ginger root
1/2 cup fresh lemon juice
2 tablespoons soy sauce
1/2 teaspoon salt
Dash of MSG (optional)

Rinse oysters in salted water, drain and dip each one in vinegar. If grated *daikon* is watery, squeeze out some of the liquid so that the *daikon* is thick but not dry. Combine *daikon*, ginger, lemon juice, soy sauce, salt and MSG. Add oysters and stir gently.
Makes 4 servings

GINGER OYSTER
Kaki no Irini

16 shucked fresh oysters,
  washed in salted water
5 tablespoons vegetable oil
8 green onions or scallions
1 tablespoon slivered ginger
  root
1 clove garlic, minced
4 tablespoons *sake* (rice
  wine)
1/4 cup soy sauce
1/3 teaspoon salt
1/2 tablespoon sugar

Place the oysters in boiling water to cover and cook for 30 to 40 seconds. Drain well and set aside.

Heat the oil in a skillet or wok, and stir-fry the onions, ginger and garlic for 20 seconds. Mix together *sake,* soy sauce, salt and sugar, add to the pan with the oysters and stir-fry over high heat until oysters are thoroughly coated. Serve immediately.
Makes 4 servings

CLAMS IN MISO
Kai no Misoni

1-1/2 pounds clams in the
    shell
1 tablespoon vegetable oil
1 clove garlic, minced
1 tablespoon *sake* (rice wine)
1/2 cup *dashi*
2 tablespoons *akamiso* (red
    soybean paste)
1/4 teaspoon sugar

Soak the clams in cold, salted
water for 4 hours. Then scrub
the shells clean under cold,
running water and drain.
    Heat the oil in a skillet or
wok and stir-fry the garlic
until browned. Add the clams
and continue to stir-fry. When
the clams partially open, sprinkle them with the *sake*. Mix
together the *dashi, miso* and
sugar and pour over the clams,
stirring just enough to thoroughly coat them with the
mixture. Cover and cook over
medium heat, stirring occasionally, until the clams open
completely.
Makes 4 servings

BROILED CLAMS
Hamaguri no Karayaki

12 clams in the shell
1 egg white, lightly beaten
Salt
1/4 cup soy sauce
1 tablespoon *sake* (rice wine)

Soak the clams in cold, salted
water for 4 hours. Then scrub
the shells clean under cold,
running water and dry with a
towel.
    Dip each clam in the egg
white and sprinkle with salt.
Place them over a charcoal
fire or broil them in the oven
until they open. Mix together
the soy sauce and *sake,* and
pour a few drops on each
opened clam. Serve imme-
diately.
Makes 4 servings

STEAMED ABALONE
Mushi Awabi

1 fresh whole abalone
Salt to scrub abalone
1 teaspoon salt
3 tablespoons *sake* (rice wine)
Thinly sliced cucumber
Lemon wedges for garnish
Soy sauce

Using a flat wooden spatula,
pry abalone loose from its
shell. Cut off green edges.
Scrub blackish portion off
with an ample amount of salt.
Rinse with cold water.
    Bring water to a boil in a
steamer and place abalone
on steaming rack. Sprinkle
salt and *sake* over abalone,
cover and steam over high
heat for 20 to 30 minutes
(depending on size of abalone). Cool and slice very
thinly.
    Arrange abalone slices on a
bed of very thinly sliced cucumbers. Garnish with lemon
wedges and serve with soy
sauce.
Makes 4 servings

BOILED OCTOPUS
Tako no Nikata

Salt for washing
1 Japanese octopus or 1 leg
  of a medium United States
  octopus
4 cups water
1/2 cup *sake* (rice wine) or
  white wine
1 tablespoon salt
Dipping sauce of choice
  (following)

Sprinkle salt over octopus and wash octopus thoroughly, making sure you clean out each tentacle, too. (The salt is used to create a little abrasiveness to facilitate cleaning.) Rinse under cold, running water. Wrap the octopus in a clean dish cloth and hit with a wooden pestle to tenderize meat a little. (The Japanese octopus tend to be smaller and more tender than American octopus, so this process may not be necessary.)

Bring the water to a boil in a saucepan, then add *sake* and salt. Add octopus, cover saucepan and boil for about 15 minutes, or until a chopstick penetrates meat easily and the octopus becomes a purplish-red color. Remove octopus from water and suspend on a hook from large portion at the top of the leg. This will allow it to uncurl.

After octopus has cooled, slice into thin rounds. Discard tip of legs. Serve with one of the following dipping sauces.
Makes 4 servings

NOTE Most Japanese fish markets on the West Coast sell cooked octopus, so you may need only to slice it.

DIPPING SAUCES FOR BOILED OCTOPUS

SAUCE #1
1/4 cup *shiromiso* (white
  soybean paste)
1-1/2 tablespoons distilled
  white vinegar
1 teaspoon *sake* (rice wine)
1 teaspoon *mirin* (sweet rice
  wine)
1 tablespoon ground *sansho*
  (Japanese "pepper,"
  optional)

Combine all ingredients and mix well. Serve in small individual dipping dishes.

SAUCE #2
Fresh lemon juice
Soy sauce

Combine lemon juice and soy sauce in proportion to taste. Serve in small individual dipping dishes.

OCTOPUS SALAD
Tako no Karashimisoae

1 leg of a medium United
  States octopus, boiled
  (preceding)
Japanese rice vinegar for
  sprinkling on octopus
1 small cucumber
1 cup wakame (dried sea-
  weed), softened in lukewarm water, drained and
  cut into bite-size pieces
1/4 cup shiromiso (white
  soybean paste)
2 tablespoons sugar
3 tablespoons Japanese rice
  vinegar
1 tablespoon hot mustard,
  mixed with 1 tablespoon
  hot water

Thinly slice octopus. Sprinkle
1 to 2 tablespoons vinegar on
it. Thinly slice cucumber and
squeeze out some of the
moisture. Toss together octopus, cucumber and wakame.
Then mix together the miso,
sugar, vinegar and mustard,
add to the octopus mixture
and mix together well. Serve
as a salad.
Makes 4 servings

SEA CUCUMBERS
WITH GRATED DAIKON
Namako no Oroshi Suae

1 fresh sea cucumber
1 daikon (Japanese radish)

SAUCE
1/2 cup grated daikon
  (Japanese radish), well
  drained
2 teaspoons freshly grated
  ginger root
2 tablespoons distilled white
  vinegar
2 tablespoons soy sauce
Juice of 1/2 lemon

Sea cucumbers dissolve when
exposed to warmth so handle
as little as possible. To clean,
cut off and discard about 1/2
inch of the open end. Slit
open lengthwise and remove
innards. Place the sea cucumber in a bowl of cold water
and swish it around with a
daikon to clean. Discard water
and drain thoroughly. Slice
sea cucumber into thin pieces.
  Combine all of the sauce
ingredients with the sea cucumber in a serving bowl and
stir well. Add more soy sauce
and vinegar according to taste.
Refrigerate until ready to serve.
Makes 4 servings

NOTE   When you purchase a
fresh sea cucumber, the lemon
rind it comes packaged with
helps to keep it fresh and
firm. Sea cucumbers are slip-
pery creatures. You cannot
chew them away. When the
flavor diminishes, just swallow.
The warmth of your digestive
system will dissolve the sea
cucumbers.

IKIZUKURI/ SASHIMI
Cutting Live Fish/Raw Fish

Ikizukuri, the art of cutting live fish, is an impressive ceremony performed before diners. With dazzling speed, a master in the art presents a live fish, fillets it and then pieces it back into its original shape before it even stops twitching. That's carrying freshness to an extreme.

Sashimi (raw fish) is also considered a delicacy in Japan, and though most people don't need such fanfare to enjoy it, it's understandable how it has been elevated to a ceremonial art. Mild and refreshing in flavor, very fresh raw fish surprisingly isn't the least bit fishy tasting. No formal Japanese dinner is complete without it.

RAW FISH
Sashimi

1 pound *very fresh* filleted
    sea fish (tuna, sea bass or
    squid)
Fresh vegetable garnish of
    choice (page 71)
Dipping sauce of choice
    (page 71)

Sashimi is a simple dish to prepare and any number of sea fish can be used. (The two favorites in the United States are tuna and sea bass). It is best not to use fresh water fish, since they sometimes carry parasites. The only trick to making *sashimi* is in the cutting, which varies with the texture of the fish. Here are three different methods.

STRAIGHT CUT   This method is used for tuna and other "heavy" fish. Cut straight down across the grain of the fish in a single stroke, moving the knife toward you. Make the slices about 1/4 inch thick and 1 inch wide. (Before beginning to slice, be sure to remove and discard any dark meat; it doesn't make good *sashimi.*)

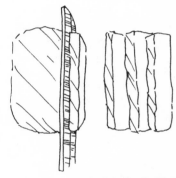

STRAIGHT CUT

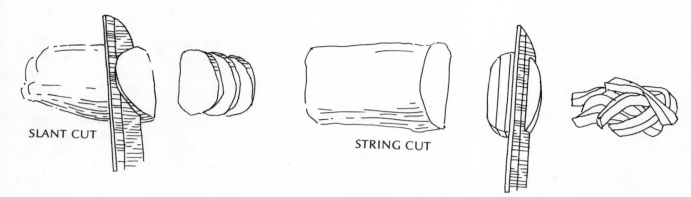

SLANT CUT   Firmer fish, such as sea bass, should be cut at slight angle into 1/8-inch-thick slices. Again, use a single stroke. As you cut each slice, lay the pieces one on top of the other, like a shingled roof.

STRING CUT   This cut is usually reserved for squid, which is very chewy, and for fish with *very thin* fillets. Use only the white tubular part of the cleaned squid. Cut straight down the length of the body, making strips about 1/8 inch wide. If using a fish fillet, cut at an angle to the length of the fillet. Since this cut looks rather sloppy if served as is, many people like to wrap the strips into neat little balls that can be unraveled as they are eaten.

continued on following page

NOTES

1.   On the West Coast, Japanese fish markets sell tuna and sea bass filleted for *sashimi*. If you are buying it elsewhere, be sure that the fish is fresh. Other fish and shellfish frequently used for *sashimi* are sea bream *(tai)*, halibut, yellow tail, mackerel, striped bass, clams, scallops, abalone, sea urchin and lobster.

If you are filleting your own fish, choose the meat close to the stomach. It tends to be fattier and less stringy than the meat by the tail.

2.   To get a neat appearance, it's important that the fish be cut in a single stroke so that it won't have ragged edges. For this you need a very sharp knife, preferably a *sashimi-bocho* (Japanese fish

slicer). Keep the fish refrigerated until you cut it to keep it firm. Better yet, put it in the freezer for about 20 minutes before cutting, but don't serve it half-frozen!

3. Our family favorite is abalone *sashimi*. It's wonderful with a little lemon and soy sauce. If you try it, cut it into transparent slices.

GARNISHES
Sashimi is traditionally served with thinly sliced or grated raw vegetables. Some favorites are *daikon* (Japanese radish), lettuce, *myoga* (a type of Japanese ginger), cucumber, *shiso* (beefsteak leaves) or *wakame* (dried seaweed). Take your pick.
Makes 4 servings

DIPPING SAUCES
FOR SASHIMI

The following dipping sauces are sufficient for serving four persons.

SAUCE #1
2 tablespoons *wasabi* (Japanese horseradish powder)
2 teaspoons cold water
Soy sauce

Mix the *wasabi* and the water until it forms a wet, thick paste. Put a dab in each of 4 individual dipping dishes. Before eating, mix *wasabi* with a little soy sauce, then dip the *sashimi* in it.

SAUCE #2
2 tablespoons *wasabi* (Japanese horseradish powder)
2 teaspoons cold water
1/2 cup grated *daikon* (Japanese radish)
Soy sauce

Mix the *wasabi* and the water until it forms a wet, thick paste. Let it sit for about 2 minutes, then mix thoroughly with the grated *daikon*. The sauce should be a refreshing green color. Divide into 4 individual dipping dishes. Before eating, mix with a little soy sauce, then dip *sashimi* in it.

SAUCE #3
Fresh lemon juice
Soy sauce

This dip is as simple as they come. Use the proportions that suit your taste. This combination tastes best with squid, clams and abalone.

Tempura

DEEP-FRIED SEAFOOD AND VEGETABLES

Interestingly enough, *tempura,* one of the most popular Japanese dishes, isn't truly Japanese. Early Japanese cooking methods were all water based, primarily steaming, boiling and braising. The use of oils and deep-frying was introduced by foreign traders. In fact, deep-fried seafood was introduced to Japan sometime in the sixteenth century by the Portuguese. The name *tempura* comes from the Latin name *Quattuor Tempora,* a Catholic holy day when followers were supposed to abstain from eating meat. On this day, the Portuguese cooked seafood in place of the meat in their diet. The Japanese adapted this Portuguese dish to their own taste, lightening the batter to a feathery crispness.

Westerners often marvel at the airy lightness of the *tempura* batter, thinking there is some deep secret involved. But *tempura* is really quite easy to make if you keep a few simple techniques in mind.

1. The vegetable oil should be fresh. You can add a little Oriental-style sesame-seed oil, if you like. It gives a nice

aroma. The temperature of the oil should be about 340 to 360 degrees. To test the temperature, drop in a bit of batter. If it sinks halfway to the bottom and comes immediately back to the surface, the heat is about right.

2. The batter should be very thin, lumpy and cold. Use ice water (some people use cold beer to make it). The batter should be so lumpy that there are still clumps of flour. Do not make too much batter at once because it gets too heavy and thick if it sits. Better to make more batter as you go along, if needed.

3. Don't put too many ingredients in the oil at once. It reduces the temperature and causes uneven cooking.

4. Skim off loose batter from the oil from time to time so it doesn't burn.

5. Drain oil from cooked food on paper toweling or a rack before serving.

Although *tempura* batter is easy to make, you may want to buy one of the very good mixes on the market today. The above techniques still apply when using a mix.

Tempura is one Japanese dish that tastes best when served immediately. Many Japanese restaurants feature *tempura* bars where patrons can sit at a counter and a cook makes the food as they eat it. You may want to play chef and cook as your family eats—great fun for them, but you'll have to postpone eating till after they're through.

Tempura with seafood, usually shrimp or small fish, and a variety of vegetables, is a complete meal in itself. Serve it with hot rice and a clear soup.

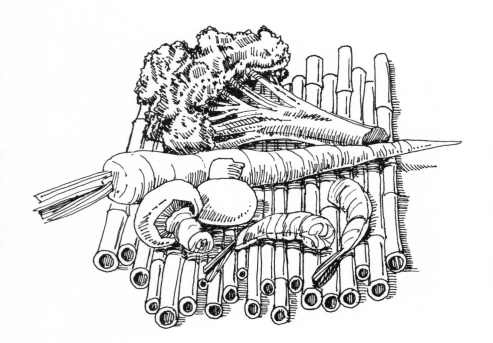

SHRIMP AND VEGETABLE TEMPURA
Ebi to Yasai no Tempura

4 small Japanese eggplants
8 Italian long sweet peppers,
  or 2 bell peppers, deseeded
Flour for coating shrimp and
  vegetables
16 shrimp, shelled with tails
  intact and deveined
2 small zucchini squash, cut
  into 1/3-inch-thick slices
8 medium fresh mushrooms
8 green beans, cut into 2-inch
  lengths
1 yellow onion, cut into 1/3-
  inch-thick slices
1 small yam or sweet potato,
  cut into 1/3-inch-thick
  rounds, parboiled 4 minutes and drained
Vegetable oil for deep-frying
Tempura Dipping Sauce
  (page 79)

BATTER
1 cup cake flour
1 teaspoon *katakuriko* (potato starch) or cornstarch
1 egg
1 tablespoon *sake* (rice wine)
1 cup ice water

Cut stem end off eggplants, then cut eggplants in half lengthwise and slit skin in several places. If using Italian sweet peppers, leave whole. If using bell peppers, cut into 1-inch-wide strips. Lightly flour the shrimp and all of the vegetables.

To prepare batter, sift together the cake flour and *katakuriko* to form a light, airy mixture. Beat the egg and then stir in the *sake* and ice water. Gently mix in the cake flour-*katakuriko* mixture. Do not stir too much. The batter should be lumpy and very thin. Begin cooking the *tempura* immediately so the batter does not sit too long. If you run out of batter before you run out of ingredients, mix up another batch.

In a pan, heat oil to a depth of 3 inches to approximately 350 degrees. Test oil by dropping in a bit of batter. If it stops midway down and rises immediately to the surface, the oil is ready.

Dip shrimp and vegetables, one at a time, into batter and carefully drop into oil. Deep-fry, a few at a time, until batter is crisp, about 3 min-utes, turning the pieces to ensure even cooking. The ingredient will float on top of the oil when it is cooked. Do not overcook vegetables that can be eaten raw. Drain on rack or paper toweling and serve immediately with dipping sauce.
Makes 4 servings

VARIATIONS Small fish, such as smelt, and other seafood, such as scallops and filleted white fish, may be added or substituted. You can substitute vegetables in season, such as celery leaves, carrots, *shiso* (beefsteak leaves), okra, broccoli, cauliflower, *gobo* (burdock root).

PRE-MARINATED TEMPURA
Ajitsuke Tempura

Salt
1 block *konnyaku* (devil's tongue jelly)
2 chicken breasts, skinned, boned and cut into bite-size pieces
2 canned bamboo shoots, sliced lengthwise 1/4-inch thick
Flour for coating bamboo shoots, *konnyaku* and chicken
Vegetable oil for deep-frying
Tempura Dipping Sauce (page 79)

MARINADE
1/4 cup soy sauce
1/4 cup *mirin* (sweet rice wine)
Dash of MSG (optional)

BATTER
1/2 cup cake flour
1/2 cup cornstarch
1 egg
3/4 cup ice water
1 tablespoon black sesame seeds, toasted (optional)

Rub salt into *konnyaku* and rinse in hot water. Slice *konnyaku* crosswise 1/4 inch thick.

Combine all of the marinade ingredients and marinate bamboo shoots, *konnyaku* and chicken for 1 hour or longer.

To prepare the batter, sift together the cake flour and cornstarch to form a light, airy mixture. Beat the egg and then stir in the ice water. Gently mix in the cake flour-cornstarch mixture and the sesame seeds. Do not stir too much. The batter should be thin and lumpy.

Drain bamboo shoots, *konnyaku* and chicken well. Dry with paper toweling. Lightly coat each piece with flour before dipping it into batter.

In a pan, heat oil to a depth of 3 inches to approximately 350 degrees. Cook *tempura* as directed for *Ebi to Yasai no Tempura* (page 74). Serve with dipping sauce. Makes 4 servings

SHRIMP-VEGETABLE TEMPURA
Kakiage

1/2 pound shrimp, shelled, deveined and chopped
2 *shiitake* (dried mushrooms), softened in lukewarm water, drained and sliced into thin strips
1/3 cup diagonally sliced green beans
1/4 cup shredded carrot
1 green onion, chopped
1/4 cup shelled green peas
Vegetable oil for deep-frying
Tempura Dipping Sauce (page 79)

BATTER
1 cup all-purpose flour
1 teaspoon baking powder
1 teaspoon salt
1/8 teaspoon MSG (optional)
1 egg
1/2 cup ice water

To make the batter, sift together flour, baking powder, salt and MSG to form a light, airy mixture. Lightly beat the egg, then mix in the water. Gently mix in the sifted ingredients. The batter should be thin and lumpy. Add the shrimp and vegetables and mix gently.

In a pan, heat oil to a depth of 3 inches to approximately 350 degrees. A few at a time, carefully drop tablespoonfuls of the shrimp-vegetable mixture into hot oil with chopsticks and poke to flatten. Cook until batter is crisp, about 3 minutes, turning them to ensure even cooking. Drain on rack or paper toweling. Serve immediately with dipping sauce.
Makes 4 servings

LOTUS ROOT TEMPURA
Renkon no Karashimisozume Age

1 medium lotus root (about 5 inches in length)
5 tablespoons *akamiso* (red soybean paste)
3 tablespoons sugar
1 tablespoon *sake* (rice wine)
1 tablespoon water
2 teaspoons dry mustard, mixed with 1-1/2 teaspoons hot water
Flour for coating lotus root
Vegetable oil for deep-frying
Parsley sprigs for garnish

BATTER

1/2 cup cake flour
3 tablespoons cornstarch
1 egg, beaten
3 to 4 tablespoons ice water

Peel the lotus root, cut into thirds crosswise and soak in cold water to cover for about 15 minutes. (This soaking will crisp the lotus root and prevent it from discoloring.) Then cook the lotus root in boiling water for 2 minutes. Drain and place in cold water again.

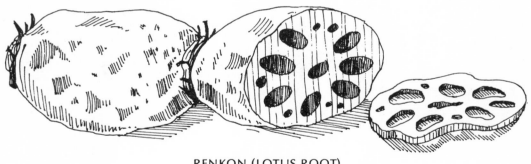

RENKON (LOTUS ROOT)

In a small saucepan, mix together the *miso,* sugar, *sake* and water. Stir constantly over low heat until the mixture is slightly thicker than *miso.* Mix in the mustard. Remove from the heat and cool slightly.

Drain the lotus root and wipe dry with paper toweling or cloth. Flour thoroughly. Fill the lotus root holes with the *miso* mixture. Flour thoroughly again.

To make the batter, sift the flour and cornstarch together twice. Stir in the egg and enough ice water to make a thin batter. Batter should be slightly lumpy.

In a pan, heat oil to a depth of 3 inches to 350 degrees. Dip the lotus root into the batter, slide into the oil and deep-fry for about 3 to 4 minutes, or until golden brown. Drain on paper toweling, then slice the lotus root into 1/4-inch-thick rounds. Arrange on a platter and garnish with parsley sprigs.
Makes 4 servings

TEMPURA DIPPING SAUCE

3/4 cup *dashi*
1/4 cup soy sauce
1/4 cup *mirin* (sweet rice wine)

Combine all of the ingredients in a small saucepan and bring to a boil. Serve the sauce in small individual bowls with any kind of *tempura.*
Makes 4 servings

NOTE *Momiji Oroshi* (page 101), grated *daikon* and chili pepper, is often served with *tempura* sauce for diners to add to taste.

Niku
MEATS

The practice of eating meat was introduced to Japan around the fifteenth century by Portuguese and Dutch traders, but for the most part, the Japanese found the idea repugnant and stuck to their basic vegetable and fish diet. Zen Buddhism and its practice of *shojin ryori* (vegetarian cooking) had been a strong influence since around the sixth century.

However, the people around the port town of Nagasaki where the traders were based tried eating the meat that was so pleasing to foreigners and liked it. Many of the early meat dishes originated in the Nagasaki area.

Still, the practice of eating meat as a main dish, rather than as an ingredient in a dish, is recent. Now that the Japanese have discovered meat, they are adapting it to their particular taste.

Since the Japanese eat only with chopsticks, not forks and knives, meat should be cut into bite-size pieces before serving.

MIXED GRILL
Teppan Yaki

1 pound beef sirloin or tenderloin, sliced in pieces
approximately 1/4 inch
thick, 1-1/2 inches wide
and 4 inches long
8 large shrimp, shelled and
deveined
1 yellow onion, cut into 1/4-
inch-thick rounds
2 bell peppers, quartered
and deseeded
2 medium zucchini squash,
halved and sliced length-
wise 1/4 inch thick
8 large fresh mushrooms,
halved
1 pound fresh bean sprouts
4 tablespoons butter

DIPPING SAUCE
3 tablespoons white sesame
seeds, toasted and chopped
3/4 cup soy sauce
3/4 cup distilled white vinegar
1/8 teaspoon MSG (optional)
1/2 teaspoon freshly grated
ginger root
1 cup grated *daikon* (Japanese radish)

Arrange the beef, shrimp and
vegetables on a platter. To
make the dipping sauce, mix
together the sesame seeds,
soy sauce, vinegar, and MSG.
Combine the ginger and *daikon,*
and divide equally among 4
small individual dishes. Pour
the soy sauce mixture over
the ginger and *daikon.*

This dish should be cooked
at the table. Using a table
griddle or electric skillet set
at 350 degrees, melt some of
the butter. Grill portions of
the beef, shrimp and vegetables, adjusting the temperature if the pan seems too hot.
Be careful not to overcook
the foods. Serve to the diners
and grill additional portions
as the foods are eaten, adding
butter to the pan when necessary. Salt and pepper may
be sprinkled on the foods
while they are grilling for
more flavor. Eat immediately
with the dipping sauce.
Makes 4 servings

BEEF WITH BUTTER
Batayaki

1 pound beef sirloin or tenderloin, very thinly sliced
1-1/2 yellow onions, cut into 1/4-inch-thick rounds
1/2 pound fresh mushrooms, halved
1 pound fresh bean sprouts
Dipping sauce, as desired (pages 84 to 85)
1/4 pound butter

Arrange the meat and vegetables on a large platter. Prepare one or two of the sauces and divide among 4 small individual bowls.

The dish should be cooked at the table. Using a table griddle or electric skillet set at 350 degrees, melt some of the butter. Grill portions of the beef and vegetables, adjusting the heat if the pan seems too hot. Be careful not to overcook the foods. Serve to the diners and grill additional portions as the foods are eaten, adding butter to the pan when necessary. Eat immediately with the dipping sauce.
Makes 4 servings

BROILED BEEF
Yakiniku

1-1/2 pounds beef sirloin or London broil, sliced in pieces approximately 1/4 inch thick, 1-1/2 inches wide and 4 inches long
1/2 head cabbage, separated into leaves
1 bunch green onions, cut into 2-inch lengths
1 large sweet potato, peeled and cut into 1/4-inch-thick rounds
2 bell peppers, quartered and deseeded
20 fresh mushrooms

MARINADE
2 tablespoons white sesame seeds, toasted
2 *togarashi* (dried red chili peppers), deseeded and finely chopped
1 clove garlic, minced
1/2 cup soy sauce
1/4 cup sugar
1 teaspoon distilled white vinegar
1 green onion, minced (optional)

Combine all of the marinade ingredients and marinate the meat for 15 to 20 minutes. Remove the meat from the marinade (reserve the marinade) and arrange with the vegetables on a large platter. Over a low charcoal fire (or a griddle or broiler), grill the meat to desired doneness. Dip the vegetables in the remaining marinade, and grill along with the meat. Serve immediately.
Makes 4 servings

FROM AN EIGHTEENTH-CENTURY PAINTING BY SUZUKI HARUNOBU

DIPPING SAUCES

These sauces can all be served with the preceding grilled beef dishes. Each is sufficient to serve four diners.

SESAME SEED SAUCE
(Goma Dare)

1/2 cup white sesame seeds, toasted and ground
1/2 cup *dashi*
2 tablespoons *mirin* (sweet rice wine)
3 tablespoons soy sauce
1/2 tablespoon *shiromiso* (white soybean paste)
1/2 teaspoon salt

Combine all of the ingredients and mix together well.

DAIKON SAUCE
(Oroshi Dare)

3 tablespoons grated *daikon* (Japanese radish)
2 teaspoons freshly grated ginger root
1 tablespoon distilled white vinegar
2 tablespoons soy sauce
1 small green onion, chopped (optional)

Combine all of the ingredients and mix together well.

GINGER SAUCE
(Shoga Dare)

3 tablespoons soy sauce
2 teaspoons *mirin* (sweet rice wine)
2 teaspoons freshly grated ginger root

Combine all of the ingredients and mix together well.

SESAME SEED AND SOY SAUCE
(Goma Joyu)

3 tablespoons white sesame seeds, toasted and ground
3 tablespoons soy sauce
1 tablespoon *sake* (rice wine)

Combine all of the ingredients and mix together well.

HOT MUSTARD AND SOY SAUCE
(Karashi Joyu)

2 teaspoons dry mustard,
mixed with 1 teaspoon hot
water
2 tablespoons soy sauce

Combine the mustard and
soy sauce and mix together
well.

HOT MUSTARD AND MAYONNAISE
(Karashi Mayonnaise)

2/3 cup mayonnaise
1 tablespoon dry mustard,
mixed with 1-1/2 teaspoons
hot water
1 teaspoon minced parsley

Combine all of the ingredients and mix together well.

NAGASAKI BEEF
Nagasaki Yakiniku

1/2 tablespoon *akamiso* (red
soybean paste)
1/2 tablespoon sugar
2-1/2 tablespoons soy sauce
1-1/2 teaspoons Oriental-style
sesame-seed oil
One 1-pound steak (club,
sirloin, etc.)
2 tablespoons vegetable oil

Mix together the *miso,* sugar,
soy sauce and sesame-seed
oil, and marinate the meat for
about 30 minutes. Heat the
vegetable oil in a skillet, and
brown on each side to desired
doneness. Cut into 1/2-inch-
thick slices, and serve immediately.
Makes 4 servings

TERIYAKI SPARERIBS

2-1/2 to 3 pounds pork
  spareribs

MARINADE
1/2 cup soy sauce
1/2 cup brown sugar
1/2 cup catsup
3 tablespoons honey
1 teaspoon garlic salt
2 teaspoons freshly grated
  ginger root

Place spareribs in a saucepan
filled with water. Bring to a
boil, reduce heat, cover and
simmer for 25 minutes. Drain
off water and set spareribs
aside.

Combine all of the marinade
ingredients. Marinate spareribs in marinade for at least 3
hours. Grill spareribs over a
charcoal fire or broil in a
broiler until nicely browned,
about 5 minutes on each
side. Do not let them cook
too long or they will dry out.
Makes 4 servings

DEEP-FRIED PORK CUTLET
Tonkatsu

4 slices pork tenderloin
  (6 to 7 ounces each), about
  1/2 inch thick
Salt and pepper
Flour
1 egg
2 tablespoons milk
Panko (Japanese bread
  crumbs) or regular bread
  crumbs
Vegetable oil for deep-frying
Shredded lettuce

SAUCE
1 cup catsup
2/3 cup Worcestershire sauce

Pound the meat lightly to
tenderize it and make 3 or 4
shallow cuts along the edges
of each piece to keep them
from curling while frying. (If
desired, the pork slices may
also be cut into 1/2-inch-
wide strips before cooking.)
Salt and pepper the pork and
dredge it in flour. Beat together the egg and milk, and
dip the pork pieces into the
mixture. Coat each piece
thoroughly with the *panko*.

In a pan, heat oil to a
depth of 3 inches to approximately 350 degrees. Carefully
slide 1 or 2 of the cutlets into
the oil and cook until the
panko is golden brown and
the pork is cooked, about 5
to 7 minutes. Turn once or
twice during cooking and be
careful the *panko* does not
burn. Drain on paper toweling.

Arrange the pork on a bed
of lettuce. Mix together the
sauce ingredients, and serve
with the pork.
Makes 4 servings

BOILED PORK
WITH DIPPING SAUCES
Buta Niku no Mushini

One 2-pound pork loin or
    shank, rubbed with salt and
    pepper
3 green onions, cut into
    3-inch lengths
1/8 pound ginger root,
    mashed
1/2 cup *sake* (rice wine)
1 cup water
1 pound vegetables, boiled,
    such as broccoli, asparagus,
    or cauliflower (optional)

Brown meat on all sides in a
skillet. Place the meat, green
onions and ginger root in a
large pot and add the *sake*
and water. Cover and simmer
gently for about 2 hours, or
until the meat is tender. Remove the meat and immerse
in cold water until the meat
is cool. Remove from the
water and refrigerate until
chilled.
    Slice the meat into desired
serving portions, and arrange
on a platter with the vegetables. Serve with the following sauces.
Makes 4 servings

DIPPING SAUCES
FOR BOILED PORK

SAUCE #1
3/4 cup *shiromiso* (white
    soybean paste)
2 egg yolks, beaten
2 tablespoons *sake* (rice wine)
1 tablespoon sugar
1/2 cup water
6 tablespoons distilled white
    vinegar
4 tablespoons dry mustard,
    mixed with 4 tablespoons
    hot water

Mix together the *miso,* egg
yolks, *sake* and sugar, and
then add the water. Put the
mixture in a double boiler,
place over simmering water,
and stir constantly until thickened. Remove from heat and
let cool. Stir in the vinegar
and mustard, and serve in
individual dishes.
    This dipping sauce is also
good with boiled or fried
white fish. Add more vinegar
or mustard to taste.

SAUCE #2
Wasabi (Japanese horseradish
    powder) or dry mustard,
    mixed with water to form a
    paste
Soy sauce
1 lemon, cut into eighths
    (wedges)

In each of 4 individual serving
dishes, place a small mound
of *wasabi* or mustard and
2 lemon wedges. Before eating
with the meat and vegetables,
each diner adds his own soy
sauce and mixes it with the
horseradish or mustard and
lemon juice.

PORK-STUFFED DUMPLINGS
Gyoza

3/4 pound ground pork
3 or 4 leaves nappa cabbage,
  finely chopped and moisture
  pressed out thoroughly
5 shrimp, shelled, deveined
  and minced
2 green onions (green part
  only), minced
1 clove garlic, minced
1/2-inch square ginger root,
  minced
1 canned bamboo shoot,
  minced
1 *shiitake* (dried mushroom),
  softened in 1/2 cup lukewarm water, drained
  (reserve water) and minced
1 tablespoon soy sauce
1/2 teaspoon salt
1-1/2 teaspoons cornstarch
Dash of MSG (optional)
1 package *gyoza* or *won ton*
  wrappers
Vegetable oil

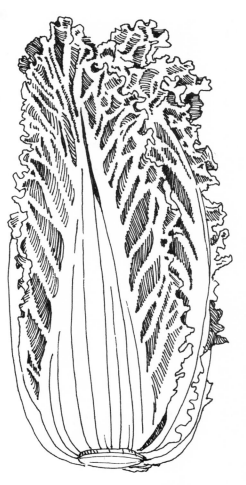

HAKUSAI (NAPPA CABBAGE)

DIPPING SAUCE
1/4 cup soy sauce
1/4 cup distilled white vinegar
1 teaspoon Oriental-style
  sesame-seed oil
Dash of hot chili oil (optional)

Combine the pork, cabbage,
shrimp, onions, garlic, ginger,
bamboo shoot and *shiitake*
and mix well. Combine *shiitake*
soaking water and soy sauce
and dissolve salt, cornstarch
and MSG in mixture. Stir into
pork mixture. The mixture
should be a gooey mass.

Put 1 heaping teaspoon of
the pork mixture on the center
of each *gyoza* wrapper. Moisten
wrapper edges with water
and fold in half, pleating top
side of wrapper so it is slightly
puckered while the bottom
side remains flat. Press edges
down to seal. Repeat with
remaining pork mixture and
wrappers.

Put 2 tablespoons vegetable
oil into a skillet and bring to
medium heat. Arrange filled
gyoza in pan with pleated

side up. *Gyoza* can be touching slightly. Cook until lightly browned on underside. Then add hot water until it *barely* covers all of the *gyoza*. Cover and continue cooking until all of the water disappears. Repeat same method with remaining *gyoza*. Arrange cooked *gyoza* on a serving platter.

Combine all of the ingredients for the dipping sauce, mix well and pour into small individual dishes. Dip *gyoza* in sauce before eating.
Makes approximately 36

NOTE Uncooked *gyoza* will freeze well, so prepare a large quantity at one time. You can thaw them and quickly cook them for an easy dinner. Be sure to separate *gyoza* with waxed or other thin paper before freezing or the wrappers will stick to one another when they are defrosted.

KAGOSHIMA ROASTED PORK
Buta no Kagoshima yaki

1-1/2-pound boneless pork roast
3 tablespoons vegetable oil
Shredded lettuce leaves or parsley sprigs for garnish

MARINADE
4 tablespoons *akamiso* (red soybean paste)
2 tablespoons *sake* (rice wine)
2 tablespoons sugar
2 tablespoons soy sauce

SAUCE
2 tablespoons catsup
2 tablespoons *mirin* (sweet rice wine)
2 teaspoons Worcestershire sauce
2 teaspoons soy sauce
2 teaspoons Oriental-style sesame-seed oil
1 teaspoon sugar
1 clove garlic, minced

To make the marinade, mix together the *miso, sake,* sugar and soy sauce. Marinate the meat in the mixture for at least 1 hour.

Heat the oil in a heavy skillet and slowly brown the meat on all sides. Remove the meat and wrap in aluminum foil. Put the meat in a roasting pan, and place in a 350-degree oven for 1 hour, or until the meat is well done.

Combine all of the sauce ingredients and mix thoroughly. Heat the mixture in a small saucepan until bubbles appear. Carve the meat into thickness desired, and arrange on a platter. Pour the sauce over the meat slices, and garnish with lettuce.
Makes 4 servings

BOILED PORK SHANK
Buta Ashi no Mizuni

Vegetable oil
1 pork shank
Salt and pepper
1 bunch parsley
1/2 cup sherry
1/8 pound ginger root,
   mashed
3 leeks
Rind of 1 lemon
2 bunches Swiss chard,
   cooked and well drained
2 tablespoons cornstarch

Heat a little oil in a skillet and brown the pork shank on all sides. Rub the meat with salt and pepper, and then place in a large pot. Add the parsley, sherry, ginger root, leeks, lemon rind and enough water to cover the meat.

Cover and cook over medium-low heat for 2 hours, or until the meat is tender. Remove the meat, and slice into desired serving portions. Strain the cooking stock and set aside.

Cut the Swiss chard into 2-inch-long pieces. Make a bed of Swiss chard on a platter, and arrange the pork slices on top. Mix the cornstarch with a little water to form a thin paste. Heat 2 cups of the reserved stock and stir in the cornstarch mixture. Continue to stir over medium heat until the consistency of thin gravy. Add salt and pepper to taste. Pour the gravy over the meat and Swiss chard, and serve immediately.
Makes 4 servings

VARIATIONS   Nappa cabbage or spinach may be substituted for the Swiss chard.

GENGHIS KHAN BARBECUE
Kabuto-yaki

This dish takes its name from the dome-shaped grill it's cooked on. The shape of the grill looks very much like the helmuts worn by Genghis Khan's soldiers.

1 pound lamb or mutton,
   thinly sliced
2 potatoes, cut into 1/2-inch-
   thick rounds
2 or 3 bell peppers, quartered
   and deseeded
1 yellow onion, cut into 1/2-
   inch-thick rounds
2 carrots, cut into 2-inch
   lengths, then halved
   lengthwise
1 small globe eggplant, cut
   into bite-size pieces
Vegetable oil, if needed

SAUCE #1

1/2 apple, peeled and grated
1 tablespoon distilled white vinegar
3-1/2 tablespoons soy sauce
2 teaspoons sugar

SAUCE #2

3 tablespoons *akamiso* (red soybean paste)
2 tablespoons white sesame seeds, chopped
1 tablespoon sugar
2 tablespoons distilled white vinegar
1-1/2 tablespoons water

Arrange the meat and vegetables on a large platter. Heat a griddle or charcoal barbecue, and, if necessary, brush with vegetable oil to prevent sticking. Grill the meat and vegetables to desired doneness. Mix together the ingredients for the sauces, and put in small individual dishes for dipping.
Makes 4 servings

FROM A DRAWING OF A VOTIVE OFFERING
MADE ON BEHALF OF ONE'S LIVESTOCK OR HORSE

BARBECUED TERIYAKI CHICKEN
Tori no Teriyaki

1 chicken, cut in half
1-1/2 tablespoons garlic salt

BASTING SAUCE
1/2 cup soy sauce
1/2 cup sugar
1/4 cup *mirin* (sweet rice wine)
1-1/2 teaspoons freshly grated ginger root

Wash the chicken and sprinkle with the garlic salt. Place the chicken in a covered bowl and refrigerate at least 4 hours or overnight.

To make the basting sauce, mix together the soy sauce, sugar and *mirin* in a saucepan, and heat, stirring until the sugar is dissolved. Mix in the ginger.

Barbecue the chicken halves over a medium charcoal fire until nicely browned and cooked. Brush on the basting sauce during the last 15 minutes of cooking. Cut the chicken into desired serving pieces. Serve hot or cold. Makes 4 servings

CHICKEN IN FOIL
Tori no Gingami Yaki

1/2 pound chicken breast, boned and cut into bite-size pieces
4 *shiitake* (dried mushrooms), softened in lukewarm water and drained
2 green onions, finely chopped
12 gingko nuts, shelled and boiled (page 54)
4 *kuri* (chestnuts), peeled and boiled (see Note)
Dash of *shichimi togarashi* (seven-spice mixture)
1/2 lemon, cut into 4 wedges

SAUCE
2 tablespoons soy sauce
1 tablespoon *mirin* (sweet rice wine)
1 tablespoon *sake* (rice wine)
1 teaspoon vegetable oil

Combine all of the sauce ingredients, and marinate the chicken, *shiitake,* onions, gingko nuts and chestnuts in the sauce for about 30 minutes. Divide the ingredients into 4 servings, and place each serving on a 7-inch square of aluminum foil. Sprinkle a dash of *shichimi togarashi* on each portion and fold the foil to securely enclose the ingredients. Bake at 375 degrees for 15 minutes, or until the chicken meat is cooked. Garnish with the lemon wedges.
Makes 4 servings

NOTE   To peel the *kuri,* slash each nut on the flat side with a sharp knife in an X shape. Soak *kuri* in warm water to cover for about 2 hours, then peel off shell and brown inner skin. Boil the peeled *kuri* in water to cover about 15 minutes, or until just tender. Drain.

FRIED CHICKEN
Tatsuta-age

4 tablespoons soy sauce
1 tablespoon sugar
2 tablespoons *sake* (rice wine)
1-1/2 pounds chicken breast, boned and cut into 1-1/2-inch pieces
3 tablespoons cornstarch
Vegetable oil for deep-frying

Mix together the soy sauce and sugar until sugar is dissolved. Stir in *sake.*
   Marinate chicken in this mixture in a large bowl for about 1 hour.
   In a pan, heat oil to a depth of 3 inches to approximately 350 degrees. Remove the chicken from the marinade and coat with cornstarch. Deep-fry until crispy and browned, turning occasionally to ensure even cooking, about 5 minutes. Drain on rack or paper toweling, and serve.
Makes 4 servings

CHICKEN LIVERS TSUKUDANI
Tori no Kimo Tsukudani

1 pound chicken livers
1 leek, cut into 2-inch lengths
2 teaspoons minced ginger root
1/4 cup *sake* (rice wine)
2 tablespoons sugar
1/4 cup soy sauce

In a skillet, combine livers, leek, ginger and *sake,* and cook over high heat for 2 minutes. Dissolve sugar in soy sauce, reduce heat and add to skillet, mixing well. Simmer until the liquid is absorbed. Remove the leek, and serve hot or cold.
Makes 4 servings

Nabemono
ONE-POT COOKING

Nabemono, which translates to "one-pot cooking," is considered a winter dish. Few Japanese homes have central heating, so on cold snowy days nothing is more appealing than to sit around a table eating your meal as you cook it. The steam from the cooker and the warmth of the hot food give a cozy feeling.

Any number of pots can be used to cook *nabemono,* from earthenware to iron skillets, but most Japanese-Americans use electric skillets to make *nabemono* at the table.

Many of the *nabemono* dishes are very similar. *Mizutaki* (meaning "boiled in water") is made with chicken or pork. *Shabu shabu* uses beef. The name comes from the sound that the beef makes while it's being swished around in the broth. In the United States it probably would be translated "slosh slosh." *Yosenabe,* meaning a "gathering of everything," uses seafood. All three of these dishes depend heavily on the dipping sauce to season the ingredients.

There are some general points to remember when making *nabemono.*

1. Prepare all ingredients beforehand and arrange them attractively on a tray so they will be handy when you sit down to eat.

2. Beef tastes best when cut very thinly. Partially freeze it beforehand so you can cut extra-thin slices or, if a Japanese market is nearby, ask them to cut it for *sukiyaki.*

3. There should be more vegetables than meat in *nabemono,* by about two parts to one.

4. Usually the meat or fish is cooked first to lend flavor to the broth. But remember also to eat it first or it will get tough and lose its flavor.

5. Put in the vegetables and ingredients that require the longest cooking time first. Vegetables like nappa cabbage will get mushy and dissolve if added too early. *Tofu* (soybean curd) should always be one of the last ingredients added because it will become hard and porous if cooked too long.

6. Don't put all the ingredients in at once. Cook only a portion at a time so that the foods can be eaten just as they are cooked.

7. Usually the initial broth is sufficient, even if you are doubling the recipe. Vegetables release a lot of liquid when cooked. However, you may find the flavor of the broth has become diluted. Add a little more broth as needed to improve the flavor.

8. In Japan, many people add *mochi* (small, plain rice cakes) to the broth after all of the other ingredients have been eaten and let it heat just until softened. At this point, the broth is rich and will give the *mochi* a delicious flavor. Or you might want to pour a little of the rich broth over your steamed rice.

9. At family-style meals where people help themselves from a single pot, it's considered proper to retrieve your serving by turning your chopsticks over and using the ends opposite from those with which you eat.

10. If you're having a leisurely meal and all the food in the pot is cooked, turn down the heat so that it will not overcook.

SUKIYAKI

For a time we translated *suki-yaki* literally—*suki* meaning "like" and *yaki* meaning "broiled" or grilled." But that didn't make sense, because *sukiyaki* falls into the *nimono* category, which means foods that are braised or boiled in liquid.

Later we found out that the *suki* the Japanese had in mind meant "plough"—grilled on a plough. In earlier days, the country was widely influenced by Zen Buddhism, which taught that it was immoral to kill a living creature. Indeed, eating land animals was considered somewhat barbaric. Still, some farmers took a fancy to the taste of meat. Occasionally they killed a wild boar or fowl and grilled it on their plough so they didn't have to carry the odor of newly slaughtered meat into their homes—hence, *sukiyaki*.

This taboo against eating land animals carried over to the end of World War II. A friend tells us that during the war, when food shortages were common, her mother received a fresh chicken. She eagerly cooked it and presented it to her family. The grandmother not only refused to eat it, but she also threw out the cutting board on which it was cut, saying it was forever tainted with the smell of animal blood.

In Western countries, meat is the main dish and vegetables are secondary. In Japanese cooking, such as *nabemono*, meat is used for flavoring, but vegetables are used in abundance. The recipes that call for a lot of meat, such as *batayaki* (beef fried in butter) and *yakitori* (skewered grilled chicken), are adaptations of Western cuisine.

2 ounces beef suet
1-1/2 pounds beef sirloin, sliced into very thin sheets
6 green onions, cut into 2-inch lengths
1/2 pound fresh or canned *shirataki* (yam noodles), cut into 1-1/2-inch lengths, boiled in water 1 minute and drained
12 fresh mushrooms
2 cakes *tofu* (soybean curd), cut into 1-inch cubes
1 can (8-1/2-ounce) bamboo shoots, sliced lengthwise 1/3 inch thick
4 eggs

SAUCE
1 cup *Kombu Dashi* (page 21)
1 cup soy sauce
1 cup *sake* (rice wine)
1/2 cup sugar

Combine all of the sauce ingredients in a saucepan and bring to a boil. Remove from the heat and set aside.

At table, heat a large electric skillet to 350 degrees. Add the beef suet and render it until the skillet is thoroughly oiled. Remove the suet. Add a small portion of beef and green onions and pour in just enough of the sauce to cover the beef. Cook for a few minutes, then start adding portions of other ingredients, keeping them separated in the pan. Do not overcook meat or vegetables.

Lightly beat each of the eggs, and put in a small individual dish. Guests may be served or may help themselves as the food is cooked. Dip each portion of food into raw egg before eating. (The egg coating keeps diners from burning their tongues on the hot food. The egg flavor cannot be tasted.) The cook adds more ingredients and sauce to the skillet as needed.
Makes 4 servings

SEAFOOD STEW
Yosenabe

12 clams in the shell
1 pound white fish fillets (sea bass or cod), cut into bite-size pieces
4-inch square *dashi kombu* (dried kelp)
1/4 cup soy sauce
2 tablespoons *mirin* (sweet rice wine)
1 teaspoon salt
1/8 teaspoon MSG (optional)
12 shrimp, shelled and deveined
1 block *kamaboko* (fish cake), sliced into 8 pieces
1 pound fresh mushrooms
2 heads romaine lettuce, cut into 2-inch lengths
1 cake *tofu* (soybean curd), cut into 1-1/2-inch cubes
2 lemons, cut into wedges

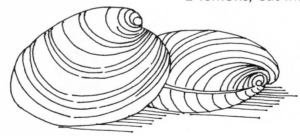

Soak clams for 4 hours in lightly salted water. Drain and scrub clam shells under cold, running water. Put clams in saucepan, add water to cover and place over medium heat until shells open. Remove clams in their shells from pan and set aside. Strain liquid and add water to make 5 cups.

At table, heat an electric skillet to 350 degrees. Make several slits along edges of *kombu,* and add with reserved clam liquid to pan. Heat just to boiling and remove and discard *kombu.* Then add soy sauce, *mirin,* salt and MSG. Finally put in all seafood, vegetables and *tofu* and boil gently until cooked.

Ladle a little soup stock from the pan into 4 individual bowls and add lemon juice to taste. Dip cooked food into this sauce before eating.
Makes 4 servings

BEEF AND VEGETABLES COOKED IN BROTH
Shabu Shabu

1-1/2 pounds boneless, tender beef steak, sliced into very thin sheets
1 medium nappa cabbage, cut into 2-inch lengths
1 can (15-ounce) bamboo shoots, sliced lengthwise 1/3 inch thick
7 green onions, cut on the diagonal into 2-inch lengths
1 bunch spinach, trimmed and leaves cut into narrow 2-inch lengths
12 fresh mushrooms or shiitake (dried mushrooms), softened in lukewarm water, drained and stemmed
1/2 pound fresh or canned shirataki (yam noodles, optional)
Dipping sauces (following)
6 cups chicken stock
4 mochi (small, plain rice cakes), or 1 cake tofu (soybean curd), cut into 1-inch cubes

Arrange beef, vegetables and shirataki, if using, on a large serving platter. Prepare sauces and divide each among 4 individual bowls.

Bring stock to a boil in an electric skillet set at 350 degrees. Holding a slice of beef with chopsticks, swish in boiling chicken stock until meat turns whitish (about 25 seconds). Do not overcook. Immerse other ingredients in the broth and allow them to cook for a few minutes, continuing to add ingredients as the cooked ones are eaten. Before eating, dip hot meat and vegetables into individual servings of one of the sauces.

If serving mochi, add after the meat and vegetables are eaten. They should be cooked only a few minutes, otherwise the mochi will melt.
Makes 4 servings

DIPPING SAUCES FOR SHABU SHABU

LEMON SAUCE
(Remon Dare)

1/3 cup fresh lemon juice or ponzu (soy-lemon juice sauce)
1/2 cup soy sauce
1/4 cup chicken stock

Combine all ingredients and mix well.
Makes approximately 1 cup

SESAME SAUCE
(Goma Dare)

1/2 cup white sesame seeds, toasted and crushed
1/4 cup shiromiso (white soybean paste)
3/4 cup dashi
1/3 cup soy sauce
2 tablespoons mirin (sweet rice wine)
Dash of MSG (optional)

Combine all of the ingredients and mix to form a creamy paste.
Makes approximately 1 cup

PORK ONE-POT
Buta no Mizutaki

1-1/2 pounds lean pork, cut
  into bite-size pieces
1-1/2 pounds fresh
  mushrooms
2 heads romaine lettuce, cut
  into 2-inch lengths
1 *daikon* (Japanese radish),
  peeled, cut into 1/3-inch
  lengths, parboiled 5 to 7
  minutes (or until chopstick
  penetrates easily) in water
  reserved from washing rice
  and drained

1 cake *tofu* (soybean curd),
  cut into 1-1/2-inch cubes
1 pound fresh bean sprouts
4-inch square *dashi kombu*
  (dried kelp)
10 cups water

SAUCE
2 cups *Momiji Oroshi*
  (following)
1 teaspoon freshly grated
  ginger root
1/3 cup *ponzu* (soy-lemon
  juice sauce)
1/3 cup soy sauce
1/8 teaspoon MSG (optional)

Prepare the meat, vegetables
and *tofu* and arrange on a
large platter.

To prepare the sauce, mix
together all of the ingredients.
Divide the sauce among 4
small individual bowls.

At table, heat a deep electric skillet to 350 degrees.
Make several slits along edges
of *kombu* and add to skillet
with water. Bring to a boil
and remove and discard *kombu.*

Add a portion each of the
pork, vegetables and *tofu* to

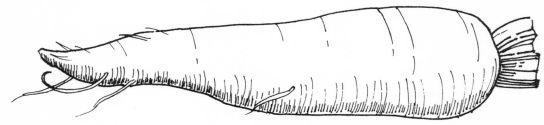

DAIKON (GIANT WHITE RADISH)

the boiling water in the skillet and cook until done. Continue adding ingredients as cooked foods are eaten. The cook may serve the diners or each individual may help himself from the skillet. Dip foods into the sauce before eating.
Makes 4 servings

GRATED DAIKON AND CHILI PEPPER
Momiji Oroshi

1 daikon (Japanese radish)
2 to 4 togarashi (dried red chili peppers)

Peel daikon and slice off stem end. Poke the large end of a chopstick into end of daikon to make 2 to 4 deep holes. Insert a togarashi into into each hole and then grate the daikon.
Makes 2 cups

CHICKEN AND VEGETABLE STEW
Umani

2 gobo (burdock roots), scraped clean and cut into 1-inch lengths
1 tablespoon vegetable oil
2 chicken breasts, boned cut into bite-size pieces
1 block konnyaku (devil's tongue jelly), torn into 1/2-inch-wide pieces
2 carrots, cut into 1/2-inch-thick rounds
2 canned bamboo shoots, cut into 1/2-inch-thick pieces
2 large or 4 medium shiitake (dried mushrooms), softened in lukewarm water, drained and quartered
4 medium sato imo (taro potatoes), peeled and cut into wedges
1-1/2 cups Niban Dashi (page 21)
1 teaspoon salt
2 tablespoons soy sauce
Dash of MSG (optional)

Boil the gobo for 15 minutes, drain and set aside. Heat the oil in a skillet, and stir-fry the chicken until golden brown. Add the konnyaku, carrots, bamboo shoots, shiitake, sato imo, and gobo; stir well and cook for 5 minutes. Combine the dashi, sugar, salt, soy sauce and MSG. Add to pan and bring to a boil over moderately high heat. Cover, reduce heat and simmer for 20 minutes, stirring occasionally. Serve hot or cold.
Makes 4 servings

CHICKEN ONE-POT
Tori no Mizutaki

28 chicken winglettes
3 quarts water
1-1/2 pounds fresh
  mushrooms
1 medium head nappa
  cabbage, cut into 2-inch
  lengths
1 cake *tofu* (soybean curd),
  cut into 1-1/2-inch cubes
1 carrot, sliced in 1/4-inch-
  thick rounds and then
  scalloped (optional)

SAUCE
2 cups grated *daikon*
  (Japanese radish)
1/3 cup *ponzu* (soy-lemon
  juice sauce)
1/3 cup soy sauce
1/2 teaspoon *shichimi togarashi* (seven-spice mixture)
1/8 teaspoon MSG (optional)
1/4 cup white sesame seeds,
  toasted and chopped

Wash and drain chicken wings, and briefly immerse them in boiling water. Combine the water and chicken in a large saucepan and bring to a boil over high heat. Reduce heat, cover and simmer for 1 hour, frequently removing foam that forms on surface. Remove chicken and set aside. Strain the broth and set aside. Arrange vegetables and chicken on a large platter.

Prepare the sauce by combining all of the ingredients and mixing well. Divide sauce among 4 small individual bowls.

At table, pour reserved chicken broth into a deep electric skillet set at 350 degrees. When broth is hot, add a portion of the chicken, mushrooms, cabbage, *tofu* and carrots, adding more as they are cooked and eaten. The cook may serve the diners or each individual may help himself from the skillet. Dip in sauce before eating.
Makes 4 servings

VARIATIONS In place of fresh mushrooms, substitute 8 small to medium *shiitake* (dried mushrooms), softened in lukewarm water, drained and stemmed.

VEGETABLE STEW
Oden

6-inch square *dashi kombu*
  (dried kelp)
8 cups *dashi*
2 teaspoons sugar
2 teaspoons salt
3 tablespoons soy sauce
3 tablespoons *mirin*
  (sweet rice wine)
1 *daikon* (Japanese radish),
  cut into 1-inch-thick rounds;
  (on one side cut a shallow
  cross)
1 cake *yakidofu* (fried *tofu*),
  cut into large
  bite-sized pieces
2 blocks *konnyaku* (devil's
  tongue jelly), rubbed with
  salt, rinsed and cut into
  large triangles

4 *chikuwa* (fried fish roll),
  cut in half
1 block *kamaboko* (fish cake),
  cut into 4 triangles
3 tablespoons dry mustard,
  mixed with 3 tablespoons
  hot water, for dipping
Soy sauce for dipping

Make several slits along edges of *kombu* and bring to a boil with *dashi*, sugar, salt, soy sauce and *mirin*. Remove and discard *kombu*. Add all remaining ingredients and simmer over very low heat for 1-1/2 hours. Serve with mustard and soy sauce for dipping.
Makes 4 servings

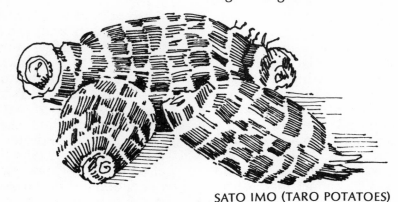

SATO IMO (TARO POTATOES)

Gohanmono
RICE

The Japanese prefer a short-grain, white rice that is moist and slightly sticky when cooked. They view rice in the same way that many Westerners view bread: It goes with every meal, even on picnics, where it is formed into small balls so that it can be picked up and eaten with the hands. An illustration of the importance of rice in the diet is the fact that *gohan*, the Japanese word for cooked rice, also means meal.

If you eat nothing else, finish your rice. It is considered impolite and wasteful to leave even a single kernel in your bowl. Rice is a gift from god, our grandmother used to say. One day she discovered a cold bowl of rice that she had forgotten. She considered it thoughtfully, and then threw it out in the field. She looked at us sheepishly and excused her actions. "I'm not wasting it. I'm just giving it to the birds to eat."

HOW TO WASH RICE

The rice should be washed at least 1 hour before cooking. Place it in the pot in which you intend to cook it. For best results, use a deep, heavy pot with heavy lid. Pour in just enough cold water to cover the rice. With your fingers, quickly stir the rice around in the water, and then immediately pour off the water. Rinse rice with several changes of water in this manner until the rinsing water remains clear. Cover washed rice with an equal amount of water, or slightly more if softer rice is preferred, then let stand for 1 hour.

HOW TO COOK RICE

Cover the pot and place over high heat until it comes to a boil. Reduce heat and continue to cook at a simmer about 15 minutes. Turn off heat and allow to stand for 12 minutes. Do not remove lid until rice is steamed, then uncover and gently fluff the rice with a wooden spatula or a fork to keep it from packing.

HOW TO USE A RICE COOKER

Many an experienced home cook in Japan would be lost if told to make rice on the stove. The automatic rice cooker is as basic as a toaster. Just wash and prepare uncooked rice in the manner described here, let stand for about an hour and press the button on the rice cooker. It shuts off automatically when done. Let rice steam for about 15 minutes longer, then remove cover and gently fluff rice with a wooden spatula.

CHESTNUT RICE
Kuri Gohan

3 cups short-grain rice,
   washed and drained
3-1/4 cups water
2 tablespoons *sake* (rice wine)
2-1/2 teaspoons salt
5-inch square *dashi kombu*
   (dried kelp)
1-1/2 cups *kuri* (chestnuts),
   shelled and skinned
   (page 93)
1 tablespoon black sesame
   seeds, toasted

Put rice, water, *sake,* salt and
dashi kombu in a heavy pot
and let stand for 1 hour.
While the rice is soaking,
soak chestnuts in water to
cover for 45 minutes. Drain
chestnuts and add to rice.
Cover and place over high
heat until it comes to a boil.
Remove *kombu.* Reduce heat
and simmer for 15 minutes.
Turn off heat and let rice
stand, covered, for 12 minutes.
Then uncover and fluff rice
with wooden spatula. Serve
in a large bowl, sprinkled
with sesame seeds.
Makes 4 servings

GREEN PEA RICE
Green Pea Gohan

2-1/4 cups *Kombu Dashi*
   (page 21)
2 teaspoons salt
1 tablespoon *sake* (rice wine)
2 cups short-grain rice, washed
   and drained
1 cup shelled green peas
   (fresh or frozen)

Mix together *dashi,* salt and
sake. Add to rice in a heavy
pot and let stand for 1 hour.
Cook rice as directed on
page 105, adding peas when
rice begins to boil. Fluff the
rice with wooden spatula and
serve immediately.
Makes 4 servings

CHICKEN AND EGG RICE
Oyako Zosui

2-1/2 cups cold, cooked
   short-grain rice
5-1/2 cups *dashi*
1 pound chicken, boned and
   thinly sliced
2 teaspoons salt
1 teaspoon soy sauce
Dash of MSG (optional)
2 eggs, beaten
1 green onion, chopped

Put the rice in cold water to
cover and stir gently until
kernels are separated. Drain
and set aside.
   Bring the *dashi* to a boil in
a heavy pot and add the
chicken, salt, soy sauce and
MSG. When it returns to a
boil, add the rice. Return to a
boil once again and, in a
circular motion, slowly pour
in the beaten eggs at the
edge of the pan. Remove
from the heat, and mix in the
green onion. Serve imme-
diately.
Makes 4 servings

BAMBOO SHOOT RICE
Takenoko Meshi

2 cups short-grain rice,
  washed and drained
3/4 cup canned bamboo
  shoots, slivered, parboiled
  1 minute and drained
1/3 cup shelled green peas
  (fresh or frozen)
2-1/4 cups *dashi*
2 teaspoons soy sauce
1 teaspoon salt
1-1/2 tablespoons *sake* (rice
  wine)
Dash of MSG (optional)

Soak the washed rice in water
to cover for 1 hour; drain
well. In a heavy pot, combine
all of the ingredients. Cover
and cook as directed on page
105. Fluff the rice with wooden
spatula and serve immediately.
Makes 4 servings

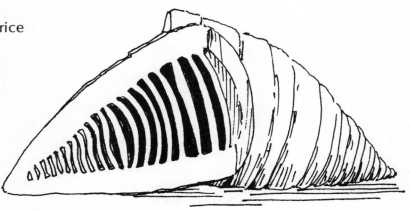

TAKENOKO (BAMBOO SHOOT)

CHICKEN FRIED RICE
Tori no Yakimeshi

1/4 cup vegetable oil
4-1/2 cups cold, cooked
  short-grain rice
1-1/2 cups cold, shredded
  cooked chicken
1/3 cup diced yellow onion
1/3 cup diced celery
1/4 teaspoon salt
 Dash of MSG (optional)
 2 eggs, well beaten
1 teaspoon soy sauce

Heat oil in skillet or wok. Stir-fry the rice until thoroughly heated, and then add the chicken, onion, celery, salt and MSG. Stir-fry for 5 minutes. Mix in the beaten eggs with the soy sauce and stir-fry until cooked and well blended. Serve immediately.
Makes 4 servings

RED RICE
Sekihan

1/2 cup *azuki* beans (red
  beans)
8-1/2 cups water
2-1/2 cups *mochigome*
  (sweet rice)
1 tablespoon black sesame
  seeds
1 teaspoon salt
Nandia leaf, parsley sprig or
  other small green leaf

Wash the beans. Place in deep saucepan with 3-1/2 cups of the water and soak overnight. Place the saucepan over low heat until it comes to a boil, then drain out water. Add the remaining 5 cups water to the beans in the saucepan, cover pot and simmer at low heat for about 30 minutes, or until beans are tender but not mushy. Drain the beans, reserving the liquid. Cover beans with a lid so they won't dry out while the *mochigome* is soaking.

Wash the *mochigome*, then drain well. Soak overnight in water reserved from cooking beans. The red bean water gives the rice an attractive pink color.

After an overnight soak, drain rice in sieve, reserving bean water again. Put rice and beans in a steamer and mix together. Make a little indentation in the center to allow steam to pass through. Steam over high heat for 30 to 40 minutes, or until rice and beans are cooked. During the cooking period, sprinkle a few times with a little of the reserved bean water. Gently loosen mixture in pan with a wooden spatula occasionally to allow steam to penetrate better.

After the mixture is cooked, place in a serving bowl. Mix together the black sesame seeds and salt, and sprinkle over the rice and beans. Place a *nandia* leaf, which symbolizes a happy occasion, in the center of the rice.
Makes 6 servings

NOTE To cook *Sekihan* in a rice cooker instead of a steamer, add 1/2 cup long-grain rice to prevent stickiness. Cook according to manufacturer's directions, using 3-1/4 cups of the water in which beans were cooked.

CHICKEN-VEGETABLE RICE
Gomoku Gohan

3 cups short-grain rice,
 washed and drained
1 *gobo* (burdock root),
 scraped clean
1 chicken breast, boned and
 skinned
4 small *shiitake* (dried mushrooms), softened in lukewarm water, drained and
 stems removed
1 carrot
1 piece *aburage* (deep-fried
 soybean curd), rinsed with
 hot water and oil pressed
 out
1-1/2 tablespoons *mirin*
 (sweet rice wine)
2 tablespoons soy sauce
1/2 teaspoon salt
1/8 teaspoon MSG (optional)
3 cups chicken stock

Soak the rice in water to cover for 1 hour, then drain and set aside. While rice is soaking, cut *gobo* into matchstick-size pieces, soak in water to cover for 30 minutes and drain. Cut the chicken meat, *shiitake,* carrot and *aburage* into matchstick-size pieces and set aside.

Bring *mirin,* soy sauce, salt and MSG to a boil in saucepan. Add the chicken meat and cook until done. Then add the remaining matchstick-cut ingredients and cook for just 30 seconds.

Put the drained rice in a heavy pot. Carefully mix in the chicken-vegetable mixture and stock. Cover and cook as directed on page 105. Fluff the rice with wooden spatula and serve immediately.
Makes 4 servings

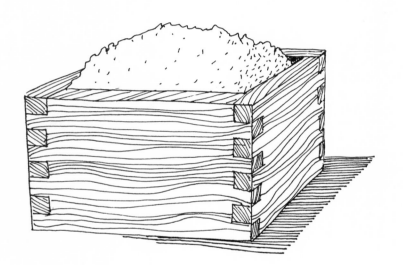

OYSTER RICE
Kaki Gohan

2 cups short-grain rice,
  washed and drained
1-3/4 cups water
1 pint shucked fresh large
  oysters, drained and cut
  into thirds
1/4 cup soy sauce
1/4 cup *sake* (rice wine)
Dash of MSG (optional)

Soak the rice in water to cover for 1 hour; drain. Carefully combine the rice, water, oysters, soy sauce, *sake* and MSG in a heavy pot. Cook as directed on page 105. Fluff rice with a wooden spatula and serve immediately.
Makes 4 servings

CRAB RICE
Kani Gohan

3 cups short-grain rice,
    washed and drained
1 can (6-1/2-ounce) crab
    meat
3 cups *dashi*
1-1/2 teaspoons salt
1 tablespoon soy sauce
1 tablespoon *mirin* (sweet
    rice wine)
1 can (4-ounce) button mush-
    rooms, chopped (reserve
    liquid)
3 eggs, beaten with 1/4 tea-
    spoon salt and 1 teaspoon
    mirin (sweet rice wine)
Vegetable oil
Watercress or parsley sprigs

Soak the rice in water to
cover for 30 minutes; drain.
Pick through the crab meat
and remove any shell fragments. Set aside 4 large pieces
of the crab meat and break
the rest of it into small pieces.
Mix together well the small
pieces of crab meat, *dashi,*
salt, soy sauce, *mirin* and
mushrooms with their liquid.
Combine the drained rice
and the *dashi* mixture in a
heavy pot and cook according
to directions on page 105.

While the rice is cooking,
heat a *tamago yaki nabe* (rectangular egg pan) over medium
heat and lightly and evenly
coat it with vegetable oil.
Pour in just enough of the
egg mixture so that it forms a
thin sheet when the pan is
tilted to evenly distribute the
egg. Cook just until set, then
flip out of pan onto a flat
surface and slice into thin
strips. Repeat with remaining
egg mixture.

Fluff the rice with a wooden
spatula and put into a large
bowl. Garnish with the egg,
reserved crab meat and watercress sprigs. Serve immediately.
Makes 4 to 6 servings

CLAM RICE
Kai Gohan

2 cups short-grain rice,
    washed and drained
1-3/4 cups water
2 tablespoons *sake* (rice wine)
1 tablespoon soy sauce
1-1/4 teaspoons salt
1/8 teaspoon MSG (optional)
1 cup fresh baby clams in the
    shell, steamed open and
    shelled, or 1 can (10-1/4-
    ounce) baby clams with
    liquid

Soak the rice in water to
cover for 1 hour. Drain. Combine the water, *sake,* soy
sauce, salt and MSG in a
heavy pot. Add the rice and
clams and mix well. Cook as
directed on page 105. Fluff
rice with a wooden spatula
and serve immediately.
Makes 4 servings

DONBURI
"Big Bowl"

Donburi, which means "big bowl," is hot rice topped with various fish, meats, eggs or vegetables. It's a meal-in-one-dish, and usually very popular for lunch.

RICE WITH CHICKEN AND EGG
Oyako Donburi

Dishes that include both chicken and egg often have oyako in the name, which translates as "parent and child."

1 chicken breast, boned, skinned and cut into bite-size pieces
1 cup chicken stock
1/4 cup soy sauce
1-3/4 tablespoons sugar
2 tablespoons sake (rice wine)
1/8 teaspoon MSG (optional)
1 small yellow onion, sliced into strips
2 canned bamboo shoots, sliced into strips
4 slices kamaboko (fish cake)
2 shiitake (dried mushrooms), softened in lukewarm water, drained and cut into julienne
3 eggs, well beaten
2 cups short-grain rice, washed and cooked

Simmer chicken in stock until cooked. Season with soy sauce, sugar, sake and MSG. Add onion, bamboo shoots, kamaboko and shiitake and bring to a boil. Pour in eggs and cook just until set. Divide rice among 4 donburi bowls and spoon an equal portion of the chicken mixture over each.
Makes 4 servings

RICE WITH BEEF AND ONIONS
Tanin Donburi

1/3 cup mirin (sweet rice wine)
1/3 cup soy sauce
1 cup Niban Dashi (page 21)
1/2 teaspoon sugar
Dash of MSG (optional)
1 pound beef tenderloin, sliced into thin strips
4 green onions, cut into 1-1/2-inch lengths
2 cups short-grain rice, washed and cooked (page 105)

Bring mirin, soy sauce, dashi, sugar and MSG to a boil in a saucepan. Stir in the beef and cook for about 30 seconds. Add the onions and remove from heat immediately. Do not overcook the beef or onions. Divide the hot rice evenly among 4 donburi bowls, and pour beef-onion mixture over the top. Serve immediately.
Makes 4 servings

RICE WITH EEL
Unagi Donburi

Our grandmother always told us that to stay healthy in hot weather, one should eat lots of deep-fried dishes and *tsukemono* (pickled vegetables). She said it was important for our systems to have more oil and salt in summertime.

Another tradition (or superstition) is to eat eel in summer. In Japan there is even a certain day in July, reputed to be the hottest day of the year, when everyone eats grilled *teriyaki* eel to keep up their strength for the rest of the hot, humid season.

Stores in Japan sell prepackaged grilled eel with little plastic bottles of *teriyaki* sauce, which many Japanese-Americans bring back to the States as gifts for friends. As yet, they have not been imported for sale in the United States. Cooked eel is sold in cans here, however, and it is quite good.

2 cans (3-4/5-ounce *each*) *unagi* (eel)
2 cups *dashi*
1/4 cup *mirin* (sweet rice wine)
1/4 cup soy sauce
Dash of MSG (optional)
2 cups short-grain rice, washed and cooked (page 105)
Chopped green onion for garnish (optional)

Open the cans of *unagi* and very carefully remove the paper-wrapped *unagi* from them. Unwrap the *unagi* and set them aside. Scrape any liquid from the cans and papers into a small saucepan. Add the *dashi, mirin,* soy sauce and MSG and place over low heat. Being careful not to break up the *unagi,* gently place them into the sauce and cook just until heated through. Spoon the hot rice into 4 *donburi* bowls, carefully top with *unagi* and pour sauce over. If desired, garnish with green onion.
Makes 4 servings

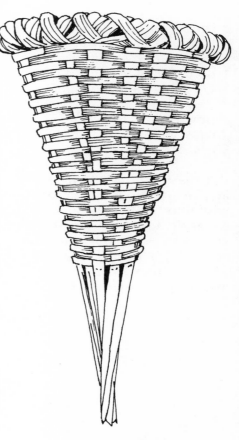

EEL TRAP

TUNA SUSHI BOWL
Tekkadon

2 sheets *nori* (dried laver),
   lightly toasted over
   low heat on stove
1 pound filleted tuna
2-1/2 tablespoons *wasabi*
   (Japanese horseradish
   powder)
2 cups *Sushi-meshi* (page 116)
Soy sauce

Cut toasted *nori* lengthwise
into quarters, then cut crosswise into 1/8-inch-wide strips;
set aside. Cut tuna across the
grain into rectangular pieces
about 1-1/2 inches long and
1/4 inch thick. (For cutting
instructions, see page 68.)

Mix *wasabi* with about 2
tablespoons cold water, or as
needed to form a thick paste;
set aside.

Divide *Sushi-meshi* among
4 *donburi* bowls and cover
rice with blanket of *nori* strips.
Arrange tuna in a rosette
pattern over the rice and
nori. Garnish the center with
a dab of *wasabi*. Serve soy
sauce in individual dipping
bowls. Mix *wasabi* with soy
sauce and dip tuna in sauce
before eating.
Makes 4 servings

RICE WITH
SHRIMP TEMPURA
Tendon Donburi

Flour
12 shrimp, shelled, deveined
   and cut in half lengthwise
8 leaves celery or parsley,
   washed and dried thoroughly
Tempura batter for *Ebi to
   Yasai Tempura* (pages
   74 to 75)
Vegetable oil for deep-frying
1/3 cup *mirin* (sweet rice
   wine)
1/3 cup soy sauce
1 cup *Niban Dashi* (page 21)
Dash of MSG (optional)
2 cups short-grain rice,
   washed and cooked
   (page 105)

Lightly flour shrimp and celery leaves and set aside. Prepare *tempura* batter. Divide celery and shrimp into 4 portions and place each portion in a bowl. Pour just enough batter over each portion to lightly but thoroughly coat the ingredients.

In a pan, heat oil to a depth of 3 inches to approximately 350 degrees. Test oil by dropping in a bit of batter. If it stops midway down and rises immediately to the surface, the oil is ready.

Deep-fry the portions, one at a time, in the oil. The ingredients should be spread out so they are in one layer, but remain joined. When one side is cooked, turn over and cook other side. Drain on paper toweling or rack.

Mix together *mirin*, soy sauce, *dashi* and MSG in saucepan. Bring to a boil over high heat. Remove from the heat and let cool slightly.

Divide the hot rice among 4 *donburi* bowls. Pour 2 tablespoons of the *dashi* mixture over each serving of rice and then dip each *tempura* portion in the remaining *dashi* mixture and place on top of rice. Pour remaining *dashi* mixture evenly over each portion and serve immediately. Makes 4 servings

SUSHI
Vinegared Rice

Sushi, meaning vinegared rice, covers a wide assortment of dishes. Home cooks most often make *makizushi,* vinegared rice with vegetables and seafood filling rolled with *nori* (dried laver); *chirashizushi,* vinegared rice mixed with seasoned vegetables; *oshi zushi,* vinegared rice pressed in a mold and topped with marinated fish; and *inari zushi,* essentially *chirashizushi* stuffed into *aburage* (deep-fried soybean curd) pouches.

The one type of *sushi* home cooks rarely attempt is *nigiri zushi,* bite-size rectangles of vinegared rice topped with *wasabi* (Japanese horseradish) and raw or cooked seafood. Simple as it looks, *nigiri zushi* demands finger dexterity and a wide assortment of fresh seafoods. In Japan, *nigiri zushi* bars are as popular as pizza parlors are in the United States. Take-out *nigiri zushi* is also widespread. In the United States, *sushi* bars are cropping up on the West Coast. Fresh seafood is flown in daily from Japan and parts of the United States to make a varied menu. As a result, prices are very high.

When making *sushi,* the main point to keep in mind is that vinegared rice should be a bit chewier than plain rice and therefore requires slightly less water when boiling. It is also important that you place the hot rice in a shallow pan when mixing in the vinegar and fan constantly to cool it and bring out a nice glaze.

VINEGARED RICE
FOR SUSHI
Sushi-meshi

3 cups short-grain rice,
  washed and drained
3-1/4 cups water
1/3 cup Japanese rice vinegar
2 tablespoons sugar
1-1/4 teaspoons salt

Soak the rice in the water for at least 1 hour before cooking. Cook rice as directed on page 105.

Combine rice vinegar, sugar and salt in a saucepan, and heat, stirring until sugar dissolves. Remove from heat and let cool to room temperature.

Turn hot cooked rice into wide bowl. Immediately sprinkle vinegar mixture over rice and mix together gently but thoroughly with a wooden spatula. Be careful not to crush the rice kernels. Cool rice to room temperature by fanning to bring out a glaze on the rice.
Makes 6 cups

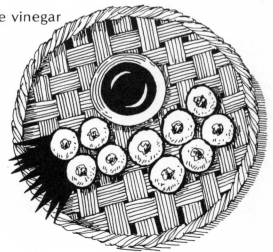

VINEGARED RICE ROLLED IN SEAWEED
Makizushi

6 cups *Sushi-meshi* (preceding)

GROUP 1
6 large *shiitake* (dried mushrooms), softened in luke-
warm water, drained (reserve
water) and stemmed
1/2 cup water reserved from
soaking *shiitake*
2 tablespoons sugar
2 tablespoons soy sauce
1 tablespoon *mirin* (sweet
rice wine)

GROUP 2
1 ounce *kanpyo* (dried gourd
shavings), dampened thor-
oughly, kneaded with
  1 tablespoon salt and softened in lukewarm water
1 cup *Niban Dashi* (page 21)
2 tablespoons sugar
2 tablespoons soy sauce
1/2 teaspoon salt

GROUP 3
2 eggs, well beaten
1/8 teaspoon salt
1/8 teaspoon sugar
1/2 teaspoon *katakuriko*
  (potato starch)
1 tablespoon *dashi,* water or
  sake (rice wine)
Dash of MSG (optional)
Vegetable oil

GROUP 4
12 leaves spinach

GROUP 5
1 can (4-ounce) *unagi* (eel)

GROUP 6
6 sheets *nori* (dried laver)

TO PREPARE
Group 1 Combine all ingredients in a small saucepan
and cook until *shiitake* are
very tender. Remove from
the heat and let cool. Slice
shiitake into 1/2-inch-wide
strips.
Group 2 Boil *kanpyo* for 3
minutes in its soaking water,
then drain. Add all of the
remaining ingredients to the
kanpyo in the pan and cook
over moderate heat until liquid
is almost completely absorbed.
Remove from the heat and
let cool.
Group 3 Combine the eggs,
salt, sugar, *katakuriko, dashi*
and MSG and mix together
well. Heat a *tamago yaki nabe*
(rectangular egg pan) over
medium heat and lightly and
evenly coat it with oil. Pour
in the egg mixture so that it
forms a sheet when the pan
is tilted to evenly distribute
the egg. Cook just until set,
then flip out of pan onto a
flat surface and slice into 6
long strips.
Group 4 Parboil spinach for 2
minutes. Rinse quickly under
cold water and squeeze out
the moisture.
Group 5 Carefully remove the
paper-wrapped *unagi* from
the can. Unwrap and discard
the paper and cut the *unagi*
lengthwise into 1/2-inch-wide
strips.

TO ASSEMBLE

Divide the *Sushi-meshi* into 6 equal portions. (*Note:* The rice should be made just before rolling so that it is still slightly warm. The other ingredients, with the exception of the egg, can be prepared a day in advance and refrigerated.)

Take 1 *nori* sheet from Group 6 ingredients and toast lightly over low heat on stove. It should not be too crisp or it will crumble when rolled.

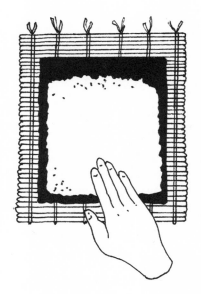

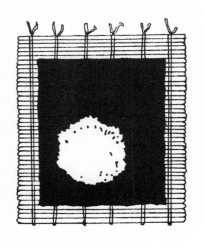

Lay *nori* on *maki-su* (bamboo *sushi* mat) or heavy dish cloth and spread 1 portion of rice evenly on *nori,* leaving a 1-inch-wide strip of the *nori* uncovered at the upper end.

Place one sixth of the *kanpyo* in a strip across the middle of the rice. Then lay a row each of one sixth of the *shiitake,* egg, *unagi* and spinach alongside the *kanpyo.*

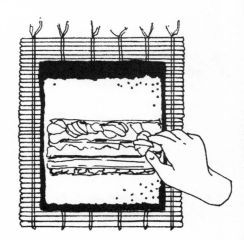

Starting from the edge closest to you, lift mat and *nori* securely together and proceed to roll away from you. When you have come to the exposed end of the *nori,* moisten it slightly with water to help seal it better when the roll is complete. Wrap mat snuggly around the rolled *sushi* to shape it. With roll still in mat, stand it on its ends so that it smooths them.

Unroll mat, remove *sushi* and set aside. Repeat same procedure to make five more *makizushi.*

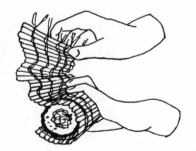

TO SERVE
With a very sharp knife, cut each roll into about 8 slices and arrange on a platter. Add a touch of green leaves, *mitsuba* (trefoil) for example, for contrast. *Makizushi* can be eaten as is, although some people like to eat it with a little *beni shoga* (pickled ginger).
Makes 6 rolls

VEGETABLE SUSHI RICE
Chirashizushi

1 small gobo (burdock root), scraped clean
1 small carrot
3 small shiitake (dried mushrooms), softened in 1-1/2 cups lukewarm water and drained (reserve water)
1/3 block kamaboko (red or green fish cake)
1/4 cup soy sauce
1 teaspoon salt
3 tablespoons sugar
1/8 teaspoon MSG (optional)
1 teaspoon sake (rice wine)
6 cups Sushi-meshi (page 116)
1/2 cup cooked green peas (fresh or frozen)

Cut the gobo, carrot, shiitake and kamaboko into slivers.
  Combine the water from soaking shiitake, soy sauce, salt, sugar, MSG and sake and heat. Add vegetables and bring to a boil. Reduce to medium heat and cook 1 to 2 minutes longer. Drain well and cool. Gently mix vegetables evenly into the Sushi-meshi. Serve on a platter and garnish with green peas.
Makes 4 servings

THIN ROLLED SUSHI WITH CUCUMBERS
Kappa Maki

3 sheets nori (dried laver), lightly toasted over low heat on stove and cut in half crosswise
3 cups Sushi-meshi (page 116)
6 strips cucumber (1/4 inch in diameter), lightly salted
4 teapoons wasabi (Japanese horseradish powder), mixed with about 1 tablespoon water to form a smooth paste

Place a half sheet of nori on a maki-su (bamboo sushi mat). Spread 1/2 cup Sushi-meshi on the nori, leaving a 1/2-inch-wide strip of the nori uncovered at the edge farthest from you. Lightly smear wasabi in a thin line across the middle of the rice. Place salted cucumber strip on the wasabi. Roll up as directed on page 118. Unroll mat, remove sushi roll and set aside. Repeat the same procedure to make five more kappa maki.
  With a very sharp knife, cut each roll into 4 pieces and arrange on a platter. Many people prefer to dip kappa maki in a little soy sauce before eating.
Makes 6 rolls

THIN ROLLED SUSHI WITH TUNA (Tekka Maki) Substitute strips of raw tuna for the cucumber.

BAGGED SUSHI
Age Zushi or Inari Zushi

8 cups milky water reserved from washing rice, or plain water mixed with 1 tablespoon salt
10 pieces *aburage* (deep-fried soybean curd), cut in half crosswise
2 cups *dashi*
2-1/2 tablespoons sugar
1 tablespoon soy sauce
1/2 tablespoon salt
Dash of MSG (optional)
1 *shiitake* (dried mushroom), softened in lukewarm water, drained and very finely slivered
1 small carrot, finely slivered
6 cups *Sushi-meshi* (page 116)

Bring milky rice water to a boil, add *aburage* and cook for 25 minutes over medium heat. Drain and rinse in warm water several times, gently squeezing out as much oil as possible each time. After last rinse, squeeze out as much liquid as possible.

Mix together *dashi,* sugar, soy sauce, salt and MSG and bring to a boil. Add *aburage* and simmer for 20 minutes, or until juices are reduced by half. Remove from heat and let cool in stock. Squeeze out liquid and carefully open to make bags. To the reserved stock, add the *shiitake* and carrot. Cook 10 minutes or until stock has evaporated. Squeeze out any liquid from *shiitake* and carrot and lightly mix into the *Sushi-meshi*. Fill each *aburage* bag with rice mixture.
Makes 20

NOTE Rice filling for Bagged *Sushi* can vary from plain *Sushi-meshi* to *Sushi-meshi* with an assortment of vegetables and/or toasted sesame seeds. Green beans and *gobo* (burdock root) are two favorites. Be sure to cut the vegetables into fine slivers and flavor them by cooking in stock.

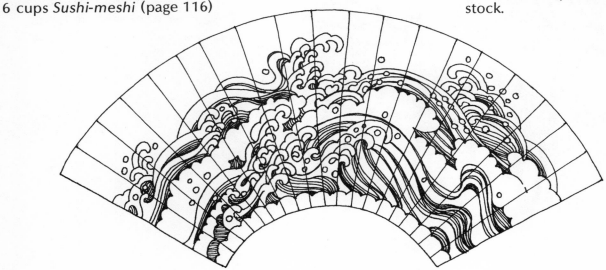

FOODS FOR THE SICK AND YOUNG

We're not about to overlook the needs of the sick or the young. *Okayu* (soft cooked rice) and *omoyu* (rice milk) are two soft rice foods that are easy to digest and rich in protein and vitamins.

When we had upset stomachs as youngsters, our Mom would make *okayu* flavored with tart *umeboshi* (pickled sour plums) or toasted *nori* (dried laver). It was also the only thing we ate after we had our wisdom teeth removed.

Omoyu, less well known in this country, is a nutritious drink for people on liquid diets or for infants. Before milk became widely available in Japan, many infants were fed *omoyu* frequently.

SOFT COOKED RICE
Okayu

1 cup short-grain rice, washed
    and drained
5 cups water
1/2 teaspoon salt

For best results, use an earthenware or Pyrex pot. Combine the rice and water in the pot. Cover and cook over high heat until it starts to boil. Lower the heat and continue cooking for 40 to 50 minutes. There should be a little water on the top. Remove from the heat and sprinkle with salt. Serve immediately.
Makes 3 cups

RICE MILK
FOR LIQUID DIET
Omoyu

1/2 cup short-grain rice,
    washed and drained
5 cups water
Salt (optional)

Proceed as directed for *Okayu,* preceding. When cooked, strain and serve just the liquid. Salt may be added to taste.
Makes 3 cups

Okazu and Tofu

**"THINGS YOU EAT
WITH RICE"
AND
SOYBEAN CURD**

OKAZU
"Things You Eat with Rice"

Okazu, which means "things you eat with rice," can be almost anything. In our family it usually meant a stir-fried meal that was quickly assembled with whatever happened to be in the refrigerator.

Once you get the hang of *okazu,* you'll find there's tremendous freedom and flexibility. You can substitute vegetables and meats for the ones given in the recipes. You can leave out or add ingredients without altering the flavor substantially. In fact, it's said that a good Japanese cook does not follow a set recipe, but knows how to cook with the ingredients on hand.

The *okazu* dishes listed here are some family favorites.

STIR-FRIED NAPPA CABBAGE
Nappa no Okazu

2 tablespoons vegetable oil
3/4 pound pork, sliced into thin strips
1 medium nappa cabbage, cut into 1-inch-wide pieces
2 tablespoons soy sauce
Salt to taste
3 tablespoons dry mustard, mixed with 1-1/2 tablespoons hot water, for dipping
Soy sauce for dipping

In a wok or skillet, heat oil and brown pork. Then add cabbage and soy sauce and blend ingredients together. Cover and simmer for about 5 minutes or until cabbage is limp. Add salt to taste.

Serve with hot mustard and soy sauce for dipping.
Makes 4 servings

STIR-FRIED EGGPLANT WITH MISO
Nasu no Misoitame

5 medium Japanese eggplants
2 cups vegetable oil
1 *togarashi* (dried red chili pepper), cut into thin rings (optional)
1/4 pound ground pork
1/2 cup thinly sliced celery
3 *shiitake* (dried mushrooms), softened in lukewarm water, drained and quartered

SAUCE
1/2 tablespoon *akamiso* (red soybean paste)
1 tablespoon *sake* (rice wine)
2 tablespoons soy sauce
1/2 tablespoon sugar
1/3 teaspoon salt

Cut off the stem ends of the eggplants. Peel them in a stripe pattern and then quarter lengthwise. Cut the quarters crosswise into 1-1/2-inch-long pieces. Soak the eggplant in water to cover for about 15 minutes, drain and dry thoroughly. Heat the oil in a wok to 350 degrees and deep-fry eggplant until it is just tender, but not soft. Remove the eggplant and drain on paper toweling.

Pour out all but 2 tablespoons of the oil in the wok, and stir-fry the *togarashi*, if using. Combine all of the sauce ingredients, add to the wok and cook 2 to 3 minutes over medium heat. Add the ground pork, celery and *shiitake*, and cook for 1 to 2 minutes longer. Mix in the eggplant and heat thoroughly. Serve immediately.
Makes 4 servings

STIR-FRIED PORK AND ZUCCHINI
Buta to Zucchini Okazu

1 teaspoon vegetable oil
3/4 pound pork, sliced into thin strips
1 clove garlic, minced (optional)
4 or 5 medium zucchini squash, cut into 1/4-inch-thick rounds
1 medium yellow onion, cut into wedges
4 whole ripe tomatoes, peeled and mashed, or 1 can (8-ounce) tomato sauce
2 teaspoons soy sauce
Salt to taste

In a skillet or wok, heat the oil and brown the meat and garlic. Add the zucchini, onion and tomatoes. Cover and simmer until the vegetables are cooked, about 6 minutes. Season with soy sauce and salt. Serve immediately. Makes 4 servings

VARIATIONS One pound green beans, cut into 2-inch lengths, may be substituted for the zucchini squash. Beef may be substituted for the pork.

STIR-FRIED BEAN SPROUTS
Moyashi no Okazu

3/4 pound pork, sliced into thin strips
1 clove garlic, minced
Vegetable oil
1/2 teaspoon salt
1-1/2 tablespoons soy sauce
1/4 cup *dashi* or water
1 medium yellow onion, cut into wedges
1 cake *tofu* (soybean curd), cut into 1-inch cubes
1-1/2 pounds fresh bean sprouts
2 teaspoons cornstarch

Heat a wok or skillet, and brown the pork with the garlic. If pork is very lean, use a little oil to prevent burning. When the pork is cooked, add the salt, soy sauce and *dashi*.

Add the onion and *tofu* and heat until warmed through. Quickly mix in the bean sprouts, and cook just until limp. Mix the cornstarch with a little water to form a thin paste and pour into the pan. Stir-fry until juices have thickened, then remove from the heat. Serve immediately. Makes 4 servings

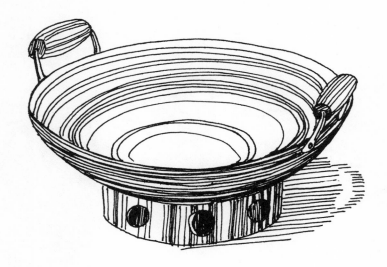

TOFU
Soybean Curd

High in protein, calcium and B vitamins, yet low in fat, *tofu* is made from soybean curds and has the consistency of firm custard. Its flavor is almost bland, but that's what makes it a welcome addition

to any dish. Moist and porous in texture and neutral in taste, it readily takes on the flavor of the other ingredients and sauces.

The Japanese use *tofu* in almost everything. They eat it cold with a little soy sauce and grated ginger, hot in *sukiyaki,* or ground up in *shiro-ae* (dressing for vegetables).

There are two things you should remember about *tofu,* though. It is perishable, so keep it in the refrigerator covered with water. If you change the water every day, the *tofu* should last for about five days. When it gets too old, it develops a sour taste and odor.

The other point is that you must not cook *tofu* too long, or it will become hard and very porous.

SAUCES FOR COLD TOFU

1 cake *tofu* (soybean curd), well drained

Carefully cut the *tofu* into cubes or into quarters. Place in individual serving dishes, and top with one of the following sauces.

SAUCE #1
1 teaspoon freshly grated ginger root
1 green onion, finely chopped
1/4 sheet *nori* (dried laver), lightly toasted over low heat on the stove and slivered
MSG
Soy sauce

Divide the ginger root, green onion and *nori* into 4 portions. Sprinkle a dash of MSG on each *tofu* serving, and top each with a ginger root, green onion and *nori* portion. Diners may pour on their own soy sauce.

SAUCE #2
2 *umeboshi* (pickled Japanese plums), deseeded and mashed
1/8 teaspoon MSG (optional)
1 green onion, finely chopped (optional)
1/4 sheet *nori* (dried laver), lightly toasted over low heat on the stove and slivered (optional)
Soy sauce

Mix together *umeboshi* and MSG, divide mixture into 4 portions and place a portion on each *tofu* serving. If desired, top with the green onion and/or *nori*. Diners may pour on their own soy sauce.
Makes 4 servings

SNOW PEAS AND TOFU
Saya-endo to Tofu

Vegetable oil
1 pound pork, cut into 1-
    inch-long strips
2 *shiitake* (dried mushrooms),
    softened in 1 cup lukewarm
    water, drained (reserve
    water) and sliced
1 cake *tofu* (soybean curd)
1 small yellow onion, sliced
1-1/2 pounds snow peas
1/2 cup fresh or canned
    water chestnuts, sliced
1/2 teaspoon salt
1 tablespoon soy sauce
Dash of MSG (optional)
1-1/2 tablespoons cornstarch

In a wok or skillet, heat a little oil and stir-fry pork until cooked. Add the *shiitake* and their soaking water, *tofu,* vegetables and seasonings and bring to a quick boil. Dissolve cornstarch in a little water to form a thin paste and add to mixture. Stir-fry until juices reach desired thickness, then remove from heat. Serve immediately.
Makes 4 servings

BEEF AND TOFU
Tofu to Hikiniki

1 tablespoon vegetable oil
1 pound ground lean beef
1 medium yellow onion, cut
    into bite-size pieces
3 tablespoons soy sauce
1 tablespoon sugar
1 tablespoon *sake* (rice wine)
Dash of MSG (optional)
1 cake *tofu* (soybean curd),
    well drained and diced
1/2 cup shelled green peas
    (fresh or frozen)

In a wok or skillet, heat oil and stir-fry beef until done. Add onion and stir-fry 1 minute. Season with soy sauce, sugar, *sake* and MSG. Add *tofu* and green peas. Cook for 3 to 5 minutes or until heated through. Serve immediately.
Makes 4 servings

NOTE If ground beef is not lean, do not use oil. Drain off excess oil before adding onion.

PORK TOFU
Butadofu

1-1/2 tablespoons vegetable
    oil
1 pound pork, cut into
    1-inch-long strips
1 yellow onion, halved and
    then cut into 1/4-inch-thick
    slices

7 fresh or canned water
 chestnuts, sliced
3 *shiitake* (dried mushrooms),
 softened in lukewarm
 water, drained and sliced
1/2 cup water
1-1/2 tablespoons sugar
2 tablespoons soy sauce
1/4 teaspoon freshly grated
 ginger root
2 tablespoons *shiromiso*
 (white soybean paste)
1 cake *tofu* (soybean curd),
 cut into 1-inch cubes

In a wok or skillet, heat oil
and stir-fry pork until done.
Add onion, water chestnuts,
shiitake and water. Cook for
1 minute. Mix together sugar,
soy sauce, ginger and *miso;*
add to pork and vegetables.
Add *tofu* and simmer for
about 4 minutes. Serve immediately.
Makes 4 servings

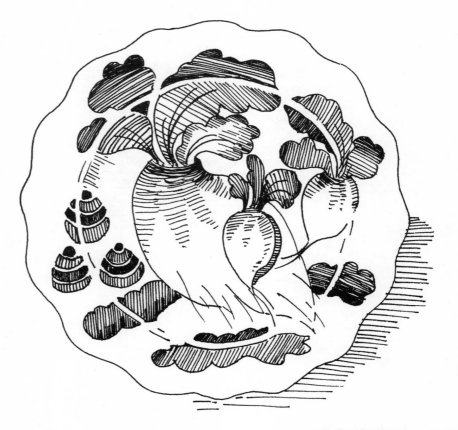

SHRIMP-TOFU PATTY
Ebi to Tofu no Yakimono

1/2 pound shrimp, shelled, deveined and finely chopped
1 cake *tofu* (soybean curd), well drained and mashed
1 green onion, finely chopped
1 egg, lightly beaten
1/4 teaspoon salt
Dash of pepper
Dash of MSG (optional)
1-1/2 cups *panko* (Japanese bread crumbs)
Vegetable oil

Combine all of the ingredients, except *panko* and oil, mix well and form into 4 patties. Coat patties with *panko*. Fry in a little oil until golden brown on both sides.
Makes 4 servings

FRIED TOFU
Yaki Dofu

1 cake *tofu* (soybean curd), well drained
1/2 cup *panko* (Japanese bread crumbs) or regular bread crumbs
1/8 teaspoon salt
Dash of pepper
Dash of MSG (optional)
1/2 cup flour
1 egg, beaten
Vegetable oil
Catsup and/or soy sauce for dipping

Cut *tofu* cake in half, then into quarters. Mix together *panko*, salt, pepper and MSG. Dredge *tofu* in flour, then in beaten egg, and finally in *panko* mixture. Fry in a little oil until golden brown on both sides. Serve with catsup or soy sauce or a blend of the two for dipping.
Makes 4 servings

BUBBLING TOFU
Yudofu

This *tofu*-based *nabemono* dish is popular throughout Japan. The secret of its success is not to cook the *tofu* too long or it will harden.

6-inch square *dashi kombu* (dried kelp)
6 cups water
2 cakes *tofu* (soybean curd), cut into 1-inch cubes
8 fresh mushrooms
12 shrimp, shelled with tails intact and deveined

DIPPING SAUCE
3/4 cup soy sauce
1/4 cup *mirin* (sweet rice wine)
1/8 teaspoon MSG (optional)
1 green onion, sliced into thin rounds
2 tablespoons freshly grated ginger root

Make several slits along edges of *kombu* and add with water to an electric skillet set at 350 degrees. Bring to a boil and remove and discard *kombu*.

To make the sauce, combine the soy sauce, *mirin* and MSG in a saucepan, bring to a boil and remove from the heat. Divide the sauce among 4 small individual bowls. Each diner may mix in onion and ginger to taste.

Add a portion each of the *tofu,* mushrooms and shrimp to the simmering water in the skillet and cook until done, adjusting the temperature if the water begins to boil. Continue adding ingredients as cooked foods are eaten. The cook may serve the diners or each individual may help himself from the skillet. Dip foods into the sauce before eating.
Makes 4 servings

Menrui
NOODLES

Japanese like to eat noodles in winter or summer. They are served either very hot in broth or very cold with dipping sauce, depending on the season.

Four types of noodle are favored. *Soba,* made from buckwheat flour, is good either hot or cold. *Soba,* which also means "nearness," is often served at the start of the New Year's holiday when loved ones return home. Some popular condiments are chopped green onions, *wasabi* (horseradish powder), grated ginger, *togarashi shichimi* (seven-spice mixture), *sansho* (Japanese "pepper"), crumbled toasted *nori* (dried laver) and toasted sesame seeds.

Udon, made from wheat flour, is traditionally served hot, often topped with *tempura,* vegetables, chicken or other foods. It is favored in winter.

Hiyamugi is a medium-size wheat noodle, usually served cold on a bed of ice, along with an ice-cold dipping sauce. The noodles are often topped with shrimp, *kamaboko* (fish cake), vegetables or chopped boiled eggs.

Somen is a very thin wheat noodle served ice cold with a dipping sauce. Since *somen* noodles are preferred in summer, the condiments served with them, such as green *shiso* (beefsteak leaves), *myoga* (a type of Japanese ginger), toasted white sesame seeds, chopped green onions or shredded *katsuobushi* (dried bonito shavings), have a refreshing flavor. The condiments should all be served in small bowls so diners can select the ones they want. To keep *somen* noodles oriented in the same direction when serving, tie them on one end with a string before boiling; when cooked, cut off string and portion where string was tied.

One last point: It's considered acceptable to make slurping noises when eating noodles. In fact, it shows you think they taste very good.

NOODLE BROTH
Kakezuyu

6 cups *dashi*
1/4 cup soy sauce
1 tablespoon *sake* (rice wine)
1 tablespoon *mirin* (sweet rice wine)
1 teaspoon salt

Combine all of the ingredients in a saucepan and bring to a boil. Use as the broth for hot noodles.
Makes approximately 6 cups

VARIATION Chicken, pork or beef stock may be substituted for the *dashi*.

COLD NOODLES WITH SHRIMP AND MUSHROOMS
Hiyamugi

1 pound dried *hiyamugi* noodles
4 medium shrimp, shelled and deveined
4 *shiitake* (dried mushrooms), softened in 3 cups lukewarm water (reserve water)
1/3 teaspoon sugar
2 teaspoons soy sauce
Vegetable oil
1 egg, well beaten
12 ice cubes
8 sprigs watercress, washed and stemmed
1 recipe *Tsuke-jiru* (page 139)

Boil noodles in a generous amount of water for about 10 minutes, or until tender. Drain in colander, rinse under cold, running water, and drain again. Set aside.

Quickly boil shrimp in water until pink and firm. Drain and place under cold, running water.

Put *shiitake* and water in which they were soaked into small saucepan and bring to boil over high heat. Add sugar and soy sauce, lower the heat and cook, uncovered, for about 20 minutes. When liquid is almost gone, turn off heat and set aside.

Lightly oil a *tamago yaki nabe* (Japanese rectangular egg pan) and place over medium heat. When pan is hot, pour in beaten egg and tilt the pan so that it forms a thin sheet. Cook over medium heat, without stirring or turning, until done. Flip egg out onto a flat surface and cut into thin strips.

Divide noodles among 4 individual bowls. Put 3 ice cubes in each bowl. Garnish each with shrimp, 2 watercress sprigs, a *shiitake*, and one fourth of the egg strips. Divide dipping sauce among 4 small dipping bowls and serve with the noodles.
Makes 4 servings

UDON WITH CHICKEN
Nabeyaki Udon

2 chicken breasts, boned
    and cut into bite-size pieces
1-1/2 teaspoons soy sauce
1-1/2 teaspoons *sake* (rice
    wine)
2 pounds fresh *udon* noodles
1 recipe *Kakezuyu* (page 135)
2 green onions, sliced on the
    diagonal
4 eggs

Marinate chicken in a mixture of the soy sauce and *sake*. Cook noodles for 6 minutes in a generous amount of boiling water. Drain in colander, rinse under cold, running water and drain again. Divide noodles among 4 individual earthenware bowls (the kind you can place on the heating element of a stove) and pour in broth. Place an equal amount of chicken and green onion on each serving of noodles. Cover and cook over high heat. When the broth comes to a boil, uncover and break an egg into each bowl. Cover and cook until eggs are cooked as desired. Serve immediately.
Makes 4 servings

FOX NOODLES
Kitsune Udon

4 pieces *aburage* (deep-fried
    soybean curd)
1 cup *Niban Dashi* (page 21)
3 tablespoons sugar
2 tablespoons soy sauce
1/8 teaspoon MSG (optional)
14 ounces dried *futonaga*
    udon noodles
2 green onions, sliced on the
    diagonal, for garnish

BROTH
4 cups *dashi*
3 tablespoons soy sauce
2 teaspoons *mirin* (sweet
    rice wine)
1/2 teaspoon salt
1/8 teaspoon MSG (optional)
2 tablespoons *sake* (rice wine)

Pour hot water over *aburage* to remove excess oil; drain. Combine *dashi,* sugar, soy sauce and MSG in a saucepan and bring to a boil. Add *aburage* and simmer until liquid is almost gone. Turn off heat and let *aburage* stand in remaining liquid until you are ready to add it to the noodles.

Cook noodles in a generous amount of boiling water for 12 minutes or until tender. Drain in colander, rinse with cold, running water and drain again. Before serving, heat noodles by pouring hot water over them, then drain well.

Combine all of the broth ingredients and bring to a boil.

Divide noodles among 4 individual bowls. Pour broth over. Halve *aburage* and place 2 halves on each bowl. Garnish with green onions. Serve immediately.
Makes 4 servings

COLD BUCKWHEAT NOODLES
Soba

1 pound dried *soba* noodles
2 sheets *nori* (dried laver), lightly toasted over low heat on stove and coarsely crumbled
1-1/2 cups *Tsuke-jiru* (following)
1 green onion, thinly sliced
1 tablespoon *wasabi* (Japanese horseradish powder), mixed with just enough water to make a thick paste

Cook *soba* in a generous amount of boiling water for about 7 minutes, or until tender. Drain in colander, rinse under cold, running water and drain again.

Divide noodles among 4 individual bowls. Garnish with *nori*. Serve dipping sauce in 4 individual bowls and green onion and *wasabi* in 2 small serving dishes. Small amounts of onion and *wasabi* may be mixed into the dipping sauce by diner, if desired. Dip noodles in sauce before eating. Makes 4 servings

NOTE *Soba* can be served hot with *Kakezuyu* (page 135).

COLD WHEAT NOODLES
Somen

1 pound dried *somen* noodles
12 ice cubes
1 green onion, finely chopped
2 tablespoons freshly grated
ginger root
1-1/2 cups *Tsuke-jiru*
(following)

Cook noodles in a generous amount of boiling water for 3 minutes. Drain in colander, rinse under cold, running water and drain again. Divide noodles among 4 individual bowls and place 3 ice cubes in each. Serve dipping sauce in 4 small bowls and green onions and ginger in 2 small serving dishes. Small amounts of onion and ginger may be mixed in with dipping sauce by diners if desired. Dip noodles in sauce before eating.
Makes 4 servings

DIPPING SAUCE
FOR NOODLES
Tsuke-jiru

2 tablespoons *mirin* (sweet
rice wine)
1/4 cup soy sauce
1 cup *Niban Dashi* (page 21)
1/4 cup *katsuobushi* (dried
bonito shavings)
Dash of MSG (optional)

Combine all ingredients in a saucepan and bring to a boil. Strain through sieve into a bowl and cool to room temperature.
Makes 1-1/2 cups (4 servings)

SOMEN SALAD
Somen no Aemono

Vegetable oil
2 eggs, beaten
2 bunches dried *somen*
noodles, cooked and drained
1 small head iceberg lettuce,
shredded
1 chicken breast, boiled until
tender, boned, skinned and
shredded
3 green onions, finely chopped
1 block *kamaboko* (fish cake),
cut into julienne
2 tablespoons chopped fresh
coriander (optional)

DRESSING
2 tablespoons white sesame
seeds
2 tablespoons sugar
1 teaspoon salt
3 tablespoons Japanese rice
vinegar
2 tablespoons soy sauce
1/4 teaspoon freshly grated
ginger root
1/4 cup vegetable oil

Lightly oil a *tamago yaki nabe* (rectangular egg pan) and place over medium heat. Pour in the egg and tilt the pan to make a thin sheet. Cook just until set, then turn out onto a flat surface. Cut into thin strips.

On a large serving platter, make a bed of the noodles, and then garnish with all of the other ingredients. Mix all of the dressing ingredients together well, and pour over the salad.
Makes 4 servings

VARIATION Any cold, cut meat may be substituted for the chicken.

Tsumamimono
HORS D'OEUVRES AND PICNIC FOODS

Zensai (hors d'oeuvres) and *bento* (picnic foods) are very similar. The Japanese concept of *tsumamimono*—things you can pick at—includes practically any dish that doesn't require bothersome broths or sauces.

In Japan when men go drinking (apparently women never do), they are served foods called *sake no tsumami*. A waitress may bring out as many as ten little dishes. One dish may contain three or four sweet black beans, another may hold two slices of raw fish, a third, pork rolled in seaweed. The portions are very small, just for sampling. Rice is never served as *sake no tsumami* because it is too filling and doesn't go well with alcoholic beverages. After the men have finished drinking and nibbling, however, they are served rice with green tea poured over *(chazuke gohan)* and some pickled vegetables.

Here we've selected some dishes that would make either good *zensai* or *bento,* but you may find many other dishes in this book that are suitable *tsumamimono* as well, such as *tataki gobo* (cracked burdock root), *tori no teriyaki* (chicken *teriyaki*), *kimpira* (stir-fried burdock root) and any number of *sunomono* dishes (vinegared things).

PORK BALLS ROLLED IN SWEET RICE
Buta no Hikiniku
no Mochigomemushi

3/4 cup *mochigome* (sweet rice)
1/3 cup soy sauce
3/4 cup water
Mustard and soy sauce for dipping

MEAT MIXTURE
1 pound ground pork
1 egg, beaten
1 tablespoon ginger root juice (extracted from grating ginger root)
2 tablespoons *sake* (rice wine)
1/2 teaspoon salt
1-1/2 teaspoons soy sauce
3 medium *shiitake* (dried mushrooms), softened in lukewarm water, drained and minced
1 green onion, minced

Wash the *mochigome* until the water is clear; drain well. Mix together the soy sauce and water, then add the *mochigome* and soak for 4 hours. Drain well.

Combine all of the ingredients for the meat mixture, mix well and shape into bite-size balls. Roll the meatballs in the sweet rice, coating evenly. Steam the meatballs over gently boiling water for about 20 minutes. Serve with mustard and soy sauce for dipping.
Makes approximately 20 balls

BURDOCK ROLL
Gobo Maki

1-pound piece flank steak
2 or 3 *gobo* (burdock roots)
Parsley sprigs for garnish
   (optional)
Mustard and soy sauce for
   dipping (optional)

MEAT MARINADE
3/4 cup soy sauce
3/4 cup sugar
1/3 cup *sake* (rice wine)
1/4 teaspoon freshly grated
   ginger root
1 clove garlic, grated

GOBO PREPARATION
2 tablespoons distilled white
   vinegar
2 quarts water
1 cup *dashi*
1/4 teaspoon salt
1 teaspoon sugar

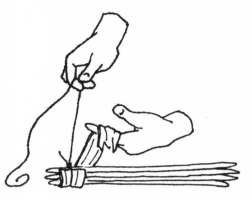

Have your butcher tenderize the flank steak. Cut the meat lengthwise into 3 strips each about 1-1/4 inches wide. Check the meat for evenness and thickness. The meat should be about 1/3 inch thick. Slice off any excess if necessary and reserve for another use. To make the marinade, mix together all of the ingredients and marinate the meat for about 3 hours.

Peel the *gobo* by scraping off the brown layer with a knife. Rinse the *gobo* in cold water thoroughly. Cut into strips each about 10 to 12 inches in length and 1/3 inch in diameter. Combine the vinegar and water and bring to a boil. Add the *gobo* and cook for about 10 minutes. Drain and rinse in cold water. Drain again thoroughly. Combine the *dashi,* salt and sugar, and heat until it boils. Remove from the heat and soak the *gobo* in the mixture for about 2 hours.

With a long string, tie together 4 or 5 *gobo* strips at one end. Then secure one end of the meat strip to the *gobo* bundle with the string, and begin wrapping the meat in a spiraling layer. Be sure to slightly overlap the meat. Spiral the string over the meat to hold in place, and tie it tightly at the opposite end. Baste the meat with the marinade. Repeat with remaining meat and *gobo.*

Broil the rolls for about 15 minutes or until done, turning and basting occasionally. Slice the rolls in 1/2-inch-thick slices. If desired, garnish with parsley and serve with mustard and soy sauce.
Makes 3 rolls

DEEP-FRIED GROUND PORK ROLLED IN SEAWEED
Buta Hiki no Isobe Age

1/2 pound ground pork
1/4 yellow onion, minced
1/2 egg, beaten
1/4 teaspoon salt
1/4 teaspoon pepper
2 sheets *nori* (dried laver), cut in half crosswise
8 strips pimiento, or 8 green beans, boiled
1/4 cup all-purpose flour
1-1/2 eggs, beaten
1 cup *panko* (Japanese bread crumbs) or cracker meal
Vegetable oil for deep-frying
Mustard and soy sauce for dipping

Combine the ground pork, onion, 1/2 egg, salt and pepper and mix together well. Put a half sheet of *nori* on a *maki-su* (bamboo *sushi* mat) and spread one fourth of the meat mixture on the *nori,* leaving a 3/4-inch-wide strip at the edge farthest from you for easy sealing. Lay 2 pimiento strips or green beans crosswise in the center, and roll as for *Makizushi* (page 117). Seal the edge with a little beaten egg. Dredge the roll in flour, dip it in the remaining beaten egg and then coat with the *panko.* Use the same procedure for the remaining *nori* and filling.

In a pan, heat vegetable oil to a depth of 3 inches to 350 degrees. Deep-fry the rolls until the meat is cooked and the *panko* is golden brown, about 3 minutes. Remove the rolls carefully, and place on paper toweling to drain excess oil. Slice the rolls into desired serving thickness, and serve with mustard and soy sauce.
Makes 4 rolls

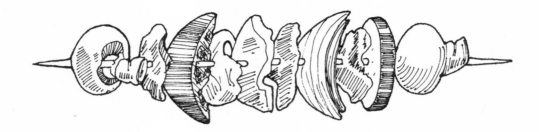

SKEWERED GRILLED CHICKEN
Yakitori

1 chicken, boned and cut into bite-size pieces
1/4 pound chicken livers, parboiled 3 minutes in salted water and drained
4 bell peppers, deseeded and cut into eighths
10 fresh mushrooms, cut in half if large
1 yellow onion, cut into bite-size pieces
4 tomatoes, cut into wedges
2 zucchini squash, cut into bite-size pieces

SAUCE
1 cup soy sauce
3/4 cup sugar
1-1/2 tablespoons *sake* (rice wine)
1-1/2 teaspoons freshly grated ginger root
1/8 teaspoon MSG (optional)
1-1/2 teaspoons cornstarch, mixed with a little water

Immerse a number of bamboo skewers in water. Remove from the water and alternately thread the vegetables and meat on the skewers. Prepare the charcoal fire or grill. To make the sauce, heat the soy sauce, sugar, *sake*, ginger and MSG until it is well blended, and then stir in the cornstarch mixture. Continue to heat until the sauce is slightly thickened.

Grill the skewered vegetables and meat until done, and then brush on the sauce before serving. If desired, return them to the fire to brown slightly.
Makes 4 to 6 servings

VARIATIONS Any type of meat or shrimp may be used in place of the chicken and chicken livers.

FRIED BEAN CURD STUFFED WITH VEGETABLES
Yasai no Maki Age

1/4 pound pork
1 tablespoon soy sauce
1 teaspoon *sake* (rice wine)
2 *shiitake* (dried mushrooms), softened in lukewarm water and drained
1 canned bamboo shoot
1/2 carrot
1/2 green onion
2 tablespoons vegetable oil
1/8 teaspoon sugar
1 egg yolk, lightly beaten
2 teaspoons *katakuriko* (potato starch) or cornstarch
4 pieces *aburage* (deep-fried soybean curd)
Vegetable oil for deep-frying
Catsup or mustard and soy sauce for dipping (optional)

Cut the pork into tiny strips, and marinate in a mixture of 1 teaspoon of the soy sauce and the *sake.* Set aside.

Cut the *shiitake,* bamboo shoot, carrot and green onion into tiny strips. Heat the 2 tablespoons oil in a skillet or wok, and stir-fry the *shiitake* and then the pork. When the pork is cooked, add the bamboo shoot and carrot. Finally, add the green onion, remaining soy sauce and sugar, and stir-fry a few seconds longer.

Mix together the egg yolk and *katakuriko.* Slit each *aburage* on 3 sides and open them up so they lie flat. Divide the pork and vegetable mixture into 4 portions and place 1 portion on each *aburage.* Wrap the mixture in the *aburage* so that each forms a triangle. Seal with the egg-yolk mixture, and secure with toothpicks.

In a pan, heat oil to a depth of 3 inches to 350 degrees. Deep-fry the *aburage* packets, a few at a time, until crispy. Drain on paper toweling and cut in half to serve. If desired, serve with catsup or mustard and soy sauce.
Makes 8 servings

MISO-STUFFED CUCUMBERS
Kyuri no Misozume

2 very straight small
   cucumbers
2/3 teaspoon salt
2 tablespoons *akamiso* (red
   soybean paste)
1 teaspoon freshly grated
   ginger root
1 teaspoon *sake* (rice wine)

Knead the cucumbers with the salt. Cut off the ends to make the cucumbers all the same length. Set aside for 10 minutes.

Push a long chopstick through each cucumber lengthwise to remove the seeds.

Mix together the *miso,* ginger and *sake.* Fill the hollow of each cucumber with the *miso* mixture by pressing it in with a chopstick. Let stand for 10 minutes until the mixture soaks into the cucumbers. Cut the cucumbers into 1-inch-thick slices and serve.
Makes 6 to 8 servings

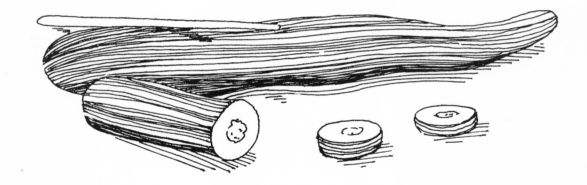

BLACK BEANS
Kuromame

This dish takes several days to prepare, but it's worth it. However, if you prefer not going to this trouble, you can buy black beans in cans at Japanese markets.

2 cups Oriental black beans
12 cups water
1 teaspoon baking soda
2 cups sugar
2 cups *kuri* (chestnuts), shelled, skinned and halved (page 93, optional)
2 tablespoons soy sauce

Soak beans overnight in 10 cups of the water and the baking soda. Then cook the beans in a covered pan over low heat for 4 to 5 hours. Check water occasionally to make sure it has not evaporated below bean level, adding water as needed. Remove from heat and rinse beans with cold water until water runs clear. Drain beans well and put in a bowl.

In a saucepan, heat sugar and the remaining 2 cups water, stirring constantly, until a light syrup forms. Let cool, then pour over beans and cover the container.

The next day, strain out syrup into a saucepan. Heat syrup and pour over the beans again. Cover and let stand overnight. Repeat for 2 consecutive days.

After 2 days, drain syrup into a small saucepan and cook over a low heat until syrup thickens. Pour over beans again, cover and soak overnight.

On final day, drain syrup into saucepan and add *kuri* and soy sauce. Cook over medium heat for 3 to 5 minutes. Let cool, then mix the syrup and *kuri* with the beans. Finally, the black beans are ready to serve. They will keep in the refrigerator for up to 1 week.
Makes approximately 5 cups

STIR-FRIED SEAWEED
Hijiki

Eat lots of seaweed if you want to prevent your hair from going gray, our grandmother used to say. It's not just an old wives' tale. Seaweed is high in calcium, protein, vitamin A and many trace minerals, including iron, potassium and magnesium. One tablespoon of cooked *hijiki* (seaweed) contains as much calcium as a glass of milk.

1 cup *hijiki* (dried bulk seaweed)
2 pieces *aburage* (deep-fried soybean curd)
1-1/2 tablespoons vegetable oil
1/2 cup *dashi*
1/4 cup soy sauce
2 tablespoons sugar

Soak *hijiki* in water for 30 minutes, then wash carefully to remove any sand. Drain well.

Pour hot water over *aburage* to remove excess oil. Drain and cut *aburage* in half lengthwise and then cut crosswise into thin julienne strips.

Heat oil in wok or skillet placed over high heat and add *hijiki*. Stir-fry over high heat until most of moisture has evaporated. If the moisture is not gone, the flavor of the *dashi* will not penetrate well. Add *aburage* and mix in well.

Mix together *dashi,* soy sauce, and sugar and add to pan. Cook over medium heat until liquid is absorbed.

This dish may be served hot or cold.
Makes 8 servings

NOTE If using instant *dashi,* make it slightly stronger than you would normally.

SKEWERED OCTOPUS AND CUCUMBER
Tako to Kyuri no Zensai

1 leg octopus, boiled (page 66)
1 tablespoon distilled white vinegar
1 small cucumber
Salt

DIPPING SAUCE
1/2 cup Japanese rice vinegar
1-1/2 tablespoons sugar
1-1/2 teaspoons salt
2 to 3 tablespoons *katakuriko* (potato starch)
1 egg yolk, beaten

Cut octopus into bite-size rings and sprinkle with vinegar. Cut cucumber into rings about the same size and sprinkle lightly with salt. Using bamboo skewers, alternately thread on octopus and cucumber rings.

Place dipping sauce ingredients, except for egg yolk, into a saucepan and cook over low heat, stirring constantly, until mixture thickens. Then add the egg yolk, mixing it in well. This mixture can be served as a dipping sauce or poured over the skewered octopus and cucumbers.
Makes 6 servings

STIR-FRIED SMALL FISH
Tazukuri

One 2-ounce package *gomame* or *iriko* (small dried fish)
3 tablespoons sugar
3 tablespoons soy sauce
2 teaspoons *mirin* (sweet rice wine)
1/4 teaspoon *sake* (rice wine)
1/4 teaspoon vegetable oil
2 tablespoons black sesame seeds, toasted

Put *gomame* in a baking pan and roast at 350 degrees for about 10 minutes until crisp.

Combine sugar and soy sauce in a large saucepan. Cook over low heat, stirring until sugar is dissolved. Add *mirin, sake* and oil and stir in well. Then put in *gomame* and stir until they are all coated with sauce. Remove from heat and fan quickly. (Fast cooling brings out glaze on fish.) Place in serving dish and sprinkle with sesame seeds.
Makes 10 servings

NOTE This dish is sometimes known as *gomame*. It is served as an appetizer or side dish, and is a must for the New Year's feast.

SWEET LIMA BEANS
Kinton

1/2 pound dried lima beans
3/4 cup sugar
1/2 teaspoon salt
2 tablespoons *sake* (rice wine)
Few drops food coloring of
    choice (optional)

Wash beans in cold water; drain. Put beans in saucepan, add water to cover, bring to a boil, reduce the heat, cover and simmer for 3 to 4 hours, or until soft. Add sugar, salt and *sake*. Continue cooking over low heat until sugar is dissolved, occasionally stirring gently to keep beans from scorching. Add food coloring to brighten appearance of lima beans. Remove from heat and serve.

This is usually served as a side dish, hot or cold. The beans will keep in the refrigerator for up to 1 week.
Makes 8 servings

EDAMAME
Soybeans

In Japan, soybeans are known as "the meat of the fields" because they contain more protein than beef, plus all the essential amino acids, yet have no cholesterol and are low in calories.

For centuries, soybeans have been Japan's principal source of protein—and the Japanese live long, healthy lives. Japanese cooks use the soybean in dozens of ways, and each time it takes on a unique flavor. Soy sauce, *miso* (soybean paste), *tofu* (soybean curd), soy milk, *okara* (soybean curd whey) and *aburage* (deep-fried soybean curd) are just some of the foods that are made from this versatile legume.

People in the United States are just beginning to discover the wonders of soybeans. As the price of meat continues to soar and cholesterol-consciousness spreads, soybeans are bound to catch on. They are very low in cost, and, oddly enough, the United States is the world's largest soybean producer.

Edamame no shioyude (boiled fresh soybeans) is a popular snack in Japan. Our grandmother remembers that soybeans ripened about the time of the beautiful August moon. Many people would boil a pan of fresh soybeans and sit outside to eat them while admiring the huge orange sphere.

BOILED FRESH SOYBEANS
Edamame no Shioyude

2 pounds fresh soybeans
  in the pod
1/4 cup salt

Wash the soybeans in their pods, and place in a *suribachi* (Japanese mortar). Sprinkle the soybeans with the salt, and rub them against the grooves of the *suribachi* to gently remove the small hairs on the pods, and to increase the salt flavor.

Bring 3 to 4 quarts of water to a rapid boil over high heat. Boil the soybeans until their color changes to a clear green. Scoop out any froth or hairs that may have floated to the top. Continue to boil 2 to 3 minutes longer; do not overcook. Drain thoroughly, and sprinkle the soybeans with salt from a shaker. Cool the soybeans quickly by fanning. This will keep their color a pretty green. Eat just the beans, not the pods.
Makes 6 servings

FRIED CASHEW NUTS
Cashew Nuts no Otsumami

1/3 teaspoon minced garlic
2 tablespoons soy sauce
1 tablespoon *shiromiso*
  (white soybean paste)
2 tablespoons sugar
1 tablespoon vegetable oil
1 cup raw cashew nuts
1 green onion, cut into 2-inch
  lengths

Mix together the garlic, soy sauce, *miso* and sugar. Heat the oil in a wok or skillet, and stir-fry the cashew nuts. Add the onion and stir-fry 30 seconds; then add the *miso* mixture. Continue to stir-fry until most of the liquid has evaporated.
Makes 1 cup

CHESTNUTS COOKED IN BITTER SKIN
Kuri no Shibukawani

30 *kuri* (chestnuts)
2-1/2 teaspoons baking soda

SYRUP
1 cup water
1 cup sugar
1/2 cup *mirin* (sweet rice
  wine)
2 tablespoons soy sauce

Soak the *kuri* in lukewarm water to cover for 20 to 30 minutes. Peel off the hard shell with a knife, but do not cut the inner brown skin.

In a large saucepan, combine the *kuri*, 1-1/2 teaspoons of the baking soda, and water to cover. Set aside for 1 day.

The next day, boil the *kuri* for 5 to 6 minutes, rinse and remove the inner brown skin. Soak the *kuri* again 1 day, adding remaining teaspoon baking soda. Then simmer 1 hour, or until tender. Scoop out any froth that might float to the top. Drain and rinse the *kuri*.

Combine the syrup ingredients in a saucepan with the *kuri* and cook over low heat for 1 hour.

The *kuri* may be stored in a jar, refrigerated, for 3 months. Makes approximately 1 quart

SWEET EGG ROLL
Tamago Maki

2 tablespoons cornstarch
1/2 cup *dashi*
1/2 teaspoon salt
1 teaspoon sugar
Dash of MSG (optional)
8 eggs, lightly beaten
Vegetable oil

Dissolve the cornstarch in the *dashi,* and then add this mixture, with the salt, sugar and MSG, to the beaten eggs. Mix well.

Heat a *tamago yaki nabe* (Japanese rectangular egg pan) over medium heat until hot and lightly coat with oil. Pour in about one third of the egg mixture and tilt the pan so that it evenly covers the bottom. When the egg is almost set but still runny on the top center surface, tilt the pan toward you and carefully roll up the egg sheet, using a spatula or chopsticks to guide it. With the roll at the end of the pan, lightly coat the pan with oil again, slide the egg roll to the opposite end and pour in half of the remaining egg, tilting the pan so that it

evenly covers the bottom. Cook and roll up as before, but this time use the first roll as the core of the second one. Repeat procedure with remaining egg mixture.

Slide the egg roll from the pan onto an *onizu* (bamboo mat), roll the mat around it and press gently. The roll should still be quite moist. Tie a string around the mat to secure it and let it stand until the egg roll is cool. Then unroll the mat and cut the rolled egg into 1/2-inch-thick rounds.
Makes 1 roll

Tsukemono
PICKLED THINGS

Pickled vegetables are a part of every meal. Like many Japanese men, our dad likes to end his meals with *chazuke gohan* (rice in green tea) and *koko* (also known as *tsukemono* or pickled things).

In the summer when there are lots of garden vegetables, our mother pickles cucumbers and eggplants in a rice-paste brine. In winter, there is always nappa cabbage or head cabbage pickled in salt and compressed with a heavy rock. *Shiozuke* (salt pickling) is an ancient method of preserving vegetables by using pressure to release the natural liquid of the vegetable. The liquid and salt work together to pickle the vegetable. There are other types of pickling brines as well, such as *miso* (soybean paste) with vinegar.

One of the most popular *tsukemono* is *umeboshi*—pickled plums. This tart red plum is considered very good for digestion. Whenever we have upset stomachs, we mash a sour plum in hot green tea and drink it. It has a soothing effect. Many Japanese travelers to Mexico carry a jar of *umeboshi* with them because they believe it will prevent them from getting "tourista." *Umeboshi* takes considerable time to make, so you should consider buying a small jar of it at the grocery.

At Japanese restaurants in the United States, *tsukemono* is served first because it stimulates the appetite. In homes, though, it is usually eaten last to finish off the rice in your bowl.

PICKLED MUSTARD EGGPLANT
Nasu no Karashizuke

4-1/2 pounds Japanese eggplants, halved and cut into 1/2-inch-thick slices
1/2 cup salt
1 cup soy sauce
1-1/2 cups sugar
1/2 cup *shiromiso* (white soybean paste)
1 cup dry mustard, mixed with 1/3 cup boiling water
1/2 cup *sake* (rice wine)
1/4 teaspoon MSG (optional)

Sprinkle the eggplant slices with salt, press with a weight and let stand overnight. The next day, drain in a colander, and then pour hot water over the eggplant. Let cool and squeeze out the excess water.

Combine the soy sauce, sugar, *miso,* mustard, *sake* and MSG, and mix thoroughly with the eggplant. Pack in sterilized jars.

The eggplants may be eaten immediately, refrigerated up to 1 month or frozen.
Makes approximately 2 quarts

PICKLED CABBAGE
AND CUCUMBER
Tsukemono

1 small head cabbage, halved
   and cut into 1/4-inch-wide
   pieces
1 cucumber, halved and cut
   into 3/4-inch-thick slices
3 or 4 tablespoons salt
3 to 5 *shiso* (green beefsteak leaves)

Mix all of the ingredients
together, gently kneading in
the salt. Press the vegetables
with a weight that is at least
5 times their combined weight
for 12 hours.
  The vegetables are ready to
eat, or may be stored in the
refrigerator up to 1 month.
Makes approximately 1 quart

TURNIP SUZUKE
Kabu no Suzuke

2 or 3 bunches turnips
Salt
2-1/4 cups water
1/2 cup distilled white or
   cider vinegar
1/4 cup sugar
1 teaspoon salt
1 *togarashi* (dried red chili
   pepper), cut into tiny squares
3-inch square *dashi kombu*
   (dried kelp), cut into
   strips

Cut the turnips in half crosswise, and then cut ends off
and discard. Make a series of
crisscrosses about 1/2 inch

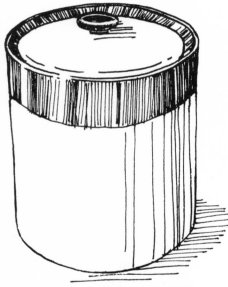

PICKLING CROCK

deep on the flesh sides of the turnips. Do not cut through to the bottom. Sprinkle with salt, and then soak for 2 hours in 2 tablespoons salt and 2 cups of the water. Drain and squeeze out the excess water. Mix together the vinegar, sugar, remaining 1/4 cup water and 1 teaspoon salt, stirring well. Combine the turnips, *togarashi* and *kombu*, and pack in wide-mouthed jars. Pour the vinegar mixture over the turnip mixture to cover, screw on lids, and store in the refrigerator for 3 days before eating.

The turnips will keep refrigerated up to 6 weeks.
Makes approximately
1-1/2 quarts

NOTE A good way to make the crisscrosses in the turnip halves without cutting all the way through is to place a chopstick on either side of the turnip half. Then as you cut the turnip, your knife reaches the chopstick before you can cut through to the work surface.

YELLOW DAIKON PICKLES
Daikon no Hawaii Zuke

6 *daikon* (Japanese radish)
Salt
3 cups water
2-1/2 cups sugar
1 cup distilled white or
    cider vinegar
3 or 4 *togarashi* (dried red
    chili peppers, optional)

Wash *daikon* and set out to dry for 2 or 3 days until limp.

Cut *daikon* into 1/3-inch-thick rounds, or quarter and cut into 2-inch-long pieces. Salt *daikon* slices. Put in pan and let sit for 1 day. Drain the liquid released from the *daikon*, but do not wash.

In a saucepan, bring water, sugar and vinegar to a boil. Pack *daikon* into hot, sterilized jars and pour in sugar-vinegar mixture to within 1 inch of top. Add *togarashi*, if desired. Seal immediately and let stand for about 10 days or until *daikon* turns yellow. It is then ready to eat. These pickles will keep up to 6 weeks in the refrigerator.
Makes 3 to 4 quarts

RICE MISO
FOR PICKLED CUCUMBERS
Dobuzuke

4 cups cold cooked short-
 grain rice
3-1/2 cups water
1/4 cup salt
4-inch square *dashi kombu*
 (dried kelp)
2 cloves garlic (optional)
3 or 4 cucumbers
Salt for cucumbers

Combine the rice, water and salt, and cook over low heat until the rice is soft and mushy. Add the *kombu* and garlic, and set mixture aside for 1 day to ferment. It is recommended that the mixture be placed in a crock or disposable container with a cover. (If the mixture seems too watery, add more cold rice, torn slices of white bread or a clean sponge to absorb the excess liquid. Be sure to remove the sponge immediately.)

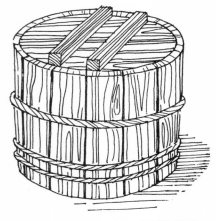

RICE KEG

If the cucumbers are large, cut them in half lengthwise. Lightly salt them, and add to the rice mixture. Be sure cucumbers are covered with rice mixture. Allow to stand 1 day, then take the cucumbers out and rinse thoroughly with cold water. Slice them into bite-size pieces, and eat with soy sauce, if desired.

The rice mixture will keep up to 10 weeks if stirred daily. Add more cold salted rice if it becomes low. Daily stirring keeps the mixture from souring.

VARIATIONS Other vegetables may be used. Halved turnips, carrots or Japanese eggplants, halved and deseeded bell peppers, or quartered cabbages are all excellent, but may need to pickle longer. Always lightly salt the vegetables before adding to the rice mixture.

BASIC SALTED SCALLIONS
Rakkyo no Shiozuke

5 pounds scallions, white part only, cleaned and washed
1 cup salt
1/2 cup distilled white or cider vinegar
1 cup water

In a large container or crock, make alternate layers of scallions and salt. The very top layer should be salt. Mix together the vinegar and water, and pour it over the scallions and salt. Cover with a plate or board, and top with a 10-pound weight. Within a few days, the water will rise and the scallions will become limp. At this time a lighter weight may be used.

After 2 weeks, the scallions will lose their bitterness and are ready to eat. Pack the scallions in jars and store up to 4 months in the refrigerator. Makes approximately 2 quarts

SWEET AND SOUR PICKLED SCALLIONS
Rakkyo no Amazuzuke

1 recipe *Rakkyo no Shiozuke* (preceding)
1 or 2 *togarashi* (dried red chili peppers)
1 cup distilled white or cider vinegar
1 cup sugar
1/2 cup *mirin* (sweet rice wine)

Follow the recipe for salted scallions. When they are ready to eat, drain them and dry on a cloth in a shady area for about 8 hours. Pack the scallions in a jar with the *togarashi*. Combine the vinegar, sugar and *mirin* and stir until the sugar is dissolved. Pour the mixture over the scallions, making sure that it covers them, screw on a lid and refrigerate.

The scallions may be eaten after 2 weeks, and will keep in the refrigerator for about 3 months.
Makes approximately 2 quarts

PICKLED SOUR PLUMS
Umeboshi

5 pounds *ume* plums
2-1/2 cups salt
1-1/2 pounds *shiso* (red
  beefsteak leaves)

Select *ume* plums that are ripe and yellowish in color, but not yet soft. Stem and wash *ume* and soak in water to cover overnight; drain.

In a porcelain crock or plastic container (do not use metal because the salt will corrode it), make alternate layers of the *ume* and 1-1/2 cups of the salt, ending with salt. Cover *ume* with a wooden board or some type of lid and place a heavy weight (about 7 to 10 pounds) on top. Let stand at room temperature for 10 days.

Remove *ume* from container, reserving liquid, and dry outdoors for 3 or 4 days on a non-metallic cookie sheet or heavy butcher paper. Do not dry in direct sunlight. Turn *ume* every day. After drying, return *ume* to reserved liquid.

The *shiso* leaves give the *ume* their red color. To prepare, combine the remaining cup salt and *shiso* leaves in a bowl and knead the leaves until they are thoroughly wilted. Drain out first black juice and knead again. Pack *shiso* leaves in a jar and add juice from soaking *ume*. Cover tightly. Place outdoors in sun for 2 days to enhance red color. Then add wilted *shiso* leaves to the *ume* and mix well. Put board back on *ume*, and top

UME (PLUMS)

with a lighter weight than used previously. Let stand for about 2 months. The *ume* will have turned a red color when ready to eat. Repack the *ume, shiso* and their soaking juice in airtight glass jars.

Umeboshi will keep as long as home-canned goods. Makes approximately 2 quarts

NOTE *Ume* usually ripen around May, but *shiso* comes out in mid-summer. If the *shiso* leaves are not ready for pickling, let the *ume* soak in the salt water until they are. The *ume* should be taken out to dry when the leaves are ready to put in.

People who make *umeboshi* usually make it in huge quantities. One year our aunt made 200 pounds. Just multiply the recipe by the weight you're pickling.

SWEET AND SOUR GINGER
Shoga no Amazuzuke

2 tablespoons canned or
    fresh beet juice (for color),
    or a few drops red food
    coloring
2 tablespoons distilled white
    or cider vinegar
2 tablespoons sugar
1/2 teaspoon salt
Dash of MSG (optional)
1/2 pound tender young
    ginger root, peeled and
    thinly sliced

Combine the beet juice, vinegar, sugar, salt and MSG. Parboil the ginger root for a few minutes. Drain and immediately put in beet juice mixture before ginger cools. Soak for at least 1 hour before serving.

If refrigerated, the ginger will keep for many months. This ginger goes well with *sushi*. It is also sold packaged at Japanese markets.
Makes approximately 2 cups

PICKLED GINGER ROOT
Beni Shoga

1/2 pound tender young
    ginger root, peeled and
    thinly sliced or cut in
    julienne
1-1/2 tablespoons salt
4 to 5 tablespoons *ume*
    (pickled sour plum) juice
2 *shiso* (red beefsteak
    leaves)
Additional *ume* juice

Place the cut ginger in a large bowl, and sprinkle on the salt and 4 to 5 tablespoons *ume* juice. Cover the bowl with a dish or board, and top with a 5-pound weight. Be sure that the weight is pressing down on the ginger root. Set aside in a cool place for 1 week, and then pack the ginger into a jar, leaving about 1 inch of head space at the top. Place the *shiso* on top, fill the jar with enough *ume* juice to cover the ginger root and leaves and screw on a lid.

Store in the refrigerator for about 1 week, and then it is ready to eat. The ginger root will keep in the refrigerator for 6 months or longer.
Makes approximately 2 cups

Okashi
SWEETS

Dessert is a Western custom. Japanese traditionally do not eat any sweets after a meal. Occasionally, they may enjoy some fresh fruit, but unless it's a *yoshoku* (foreign) dinner, they don't eat cakes or pies.

Normally fruit, such as apples, pears and persimmons, are cut in bite-sized pieces and served in individual dishes. But *mikan* (Japanese tangerines) are served whole in a bowl. Strawberries and melon are other favorite after-meal fruits.

The time when Japanese usually enjoy sweet things is with tea or for snacks. Modern-day Japanese have developed a taste for French pastries and shops selling eclairs and other delights are everywhere. Still, most Japanese don't have as much of a "sweet tooth" as Americans.

FRUIT COCKTAIL KANTEN
Mitsumame

1 stick *kanten* (agar agar)
1-1/4 cups water
1/4 cup sugar
1-1/4 cups milk
2 drops almond extract
Canned fruit cocktail or other
   desired fruit

Rinse the *kanten* and soak in
water to cover for 1 hour.
Drain, squeeze out the water
and tear into small pieces.
Dissolve the *kanten* in water
over low heat, stirring constantly. Add the sugar and
heat, stirring to dissolve sugar.
Add the milk, and heat, but
do not boil. Stir in the almond
extract, and pour into a 9- by
9-inch shallow baking dish.
Cool and cut into desired
shapes. Arrange the jelled
pieces in a bowl or individual
serving dishes, and pour on
the canned fruits. Refrigerate
until ready to serve.
Makes 6 servings

KANTEN WITH RED BEANS
Mizuyokan

1 stick *kanten* (agar agar)
1-1/4 cups water
1 cup sugar
1 cup *Koshian* (page 169)

Soak the *kanten* in water to
cover for 1 hour. Drain,
squeeze out the excess water
and tear into small pieces.
Dissolve the *kanten* in water
over low heat, stirring constantly. Add the sugar, and
heat, stirring to dissolve the
sugar. Strain the mixture, pour
back into the saucepan and
add the *Koshian*. Cook over
medium heat for 8 to 10
minutes, stirring constantly.
Pour into a 9- by 9-inch
shallow baking dish, cool and
cut into desired shapes. Refrigerate until ready to serve.
Makes 6 servings

GREEN TEA ICE CREAM
Mattcha Aisu Kurimu

1 pint vanilla ice cream
1 to 1-1/2 teaspoons *mattcha*
   (powdered green tea)

Soften the ice cream slightly,
and add the *mattcha*. Beat
the mixture until it is well
blended. Freeze until firm.
Makes 1 pint

PUFFED RICE SQUARES
Okoshi

2 cups sugar
1/2 cup water
2 cups corn syrup
1 box (8-ounce) Rice Krispies
3/4 cup smooth peanut butter

Combine sugar, water and syrup in a saucepan, and bring to a boil over low heat. Mixture should pull like taffy when tested in cold water. Warm Rice Krispies in a large pot, mixing in the peanut butter. Add syrup mixture and blend well. Pour mixture into a 9- by 13- by 2-inch pan that has been lightly greased with butter. Gently press top to smooth it. Let set for at least 30 minutes before cutting into squares.
Makes 8 to 10 servings

LICHEE NUTS AND ICE

1 can (13-ounce) lichee nuts
12 ice cubes, slightly crushed

Chill the can of lichee nuts until ready to serve. Place the contents of the can, including the syrup, in a large bowl or in individual serving dishes with the ice. Serve immediately.
Makes 4 servings

SPONGE CAKE
Kasutera

6 egg yolks
3/4 cup sugar
2 tablespoons fresh lemon
   juice
1/2 teaspoon freshly grated
   lemon rind
1 teaspoon vanilla extract
1/4 cup water
1 cup cake flour, sifted
6 egg whites
1/4 teaspoon salt
1 teaspoon cream of tartar

Let the egg yolks stand at room temperature for at least 3 to 4 hours. Beat the yolks until they are thick and lemony in color, then gradually beat in the sugar. Continue to beat while gradually adding the lemon juice and rind, vanilla, and then the water, a little at a time. Gradually blend in the flour.

In a separate bowl and with clean utensils, beat the egg whites until soft peaks are formed. Add the salt and cream of tartar, and continue beating until stiff but not dry. Fold the egg whites into the batter.

Pour the batter into a 9- by 6-inch ungreased pan, and bake in a preheated 325-degree oven for 45 minutes or until done.
Makes 6 servings

COCONUT SWEET-RICE CAKE
Coconut Mochi

1 box (1-pound) dark brown sugar
5 cups *mochiko* (sweet rice flour)
1 teaspoon baking soda
1 can (12-ounce) frozen coconut milk, thawed
2-1/2 cups water
White sesame seeds

Mix together all ingredients, except sesame seeds, in a large bowl. Then pour into a 9- by 13- by 2-inch greased pan and spread the mixture evenly. Sprinkle with sesame seeds.

Bake in a preheated 350-degree oven for 1 hour and 15 minutes. Put a pan of hot water on the lower shelf of oven while baking to create some moisture. Allow *mochi* to cool and cut into serving sizes.
Makes 8 to 10 servings

JELLO SWEET-RICE CAKE
Jello Mochi

1 box (1 pound) *mochiko* (sweet rice flour)
2-1/4 cups water
2-3/4 cups sugar
2 tablespoons Jello powder, flavor of choice
3/4 cup hot water
Katakuriko or cornstarch

Mix together well the *mochiko* and 2 cups water. Line a steamer with a cloth. Pour in mixture and steam above gently boiling water for 20 minutes. Dissolve the sugar and Jello in the hot water, boil gently for about 2 minutes, then beat it with a wire whisk into the steamed mixture. Coat a 9- by 13- by 2-inch pan with sifted *katakuriko* or cornstarch. Pour the mixture into the pan, smoothing the top. Cool thoroughly. Cut into desired shapes and sizes. Rub *katakuriko* or cornstarch on pieces to keep them from sticking together. Brush off excess.
Makes 8 to 10 servings

SWEET-RICE CAKE WITH RED BEANS
Ohagi

3 cups *Koshian* (page 169)
1 cup sugar
1/2 teaspoon salt
3 cups *mochigome* (sweet rice)
1 tablespoon sugar

Mix together the *Koshian*, 1 cup sugar and salt, and cook over medium heat, stirring, until it becomes a thick paste. Remove from the heat and let cool.

Wash the *mochigome* 1 hour before cooking, then follow the basic cooking instructions on page 105. Add 1 tablespoon sugar to the cooked rice and stir a few times with a wooden spatula.

Cut a 6-inch-square piece of taffeta cloth, get it wet and then wring it out. With wet hands, form a ball of rice about 2 inches in diameter and slightly flattened on top. Spread a 1/4-inch layer of the *Koshian* mixture on the cloth and carefully wrap it around the rice ball, coating the ball evenly. Remove the cloth. Continue to make the other balls in the same way.
Makes approximately 18 to 24

NOTE You can use any lint-free cloth, such as a tea towel, but we've found that taffeta works best. The mixture often sticks to other types of cloth.

GREEN TEA SWEET-RICE CAKE
Mattcha Mochi

1 box (1-pound) *mochiko* (sweet rice flour)
3-1/4 cups water
2 tablespoons *mattcha* (powdered green tea)
3 cups sugar
1/4 cup *kinako* (roasted soybean flour)

Mix together well the *mochiko* and 2 cups of the water. Line a steamer with a cloth. Pour in the mixture and steam above boiling water for 20 minutes.

Dissolve the *mattcha* in 1/4 cup of the water. Put the sugar and the remaining 1 cup water in a saucepan and bring to a boil, stirring to dissolve sugar. Combine *mattcha* and sugar mixtures with steamed *mochiko* and blend well with a wire whisk. Generously coat a 9- by 13- by 2-inch pan with *kinako* and pour the mixture into the pan, smoothing the top. Cool thoroughly. Cut with a cake spatula into desired shapes and sizes, and sprinkle the top with *kinako*.
Makes 8 to 10 servings

STEAMED "BUNS" WITH RED BEANS
Manju

1-1/2 cups all-purpose flour
1-1/2 teaspoons baking
  powder
1/3 cup sugar
1/2 teaspoon vegetable oil
1/2 teaspoon *sake* (rice wine)
1 teaspoon corn syrup
1/4 cup milk

FILLING
3 cups *Koshian* (following)
2 cups sugar
1/4 teaspoon salt

FROM A SEVENTEENTH-CENTURY TEA LEAF JAR

To make the filling, mix together the *Koshian,* sugar and salt, and heat, stirring until the sugar dissolves. Cool and form into 15 balls.

Sift together flour, baking powder and sugar into a bowl. Mix together oil, *sake,* syrup and milk, and mix into dry ingredients, a little at a time. Using a tablespoonful of dough at a time, form into a flat circle and place a small ball of the bean-paste mixture in the center of the circle. Encase filling with dough and press to seal. Place the balls on waxed paper until all of them have been made. Steam over gently boiling water for about 5 minutes, or until the dough is cooked. Serve in tiny paper cupcake cups.
Makes 15

RED-BEAN PASTE
Koshian

1 cup *azuki* beans (red beans)

Soak the beans in water to cover overnight. Drain, and boil the beans in clean water to cover for 2 minutes. Pour off the boiling water, add 3 cups of clean water to the beans and bring to a boil. When it comes to a boil, pour in 1 cup of cold water. Repeat this procedure 3 times. When the beans return to a boil after adding the third cup of cold water, cover, reduce the heat and simmer until the beans are soft.

Drain off any liquid and pour beans into a *suribachi* (Japanese mortar). Crush the beans to a smooth paste. Put the paste through a food mill or coarse sieve, adding water as needed so that it will go through easily. (Or you can put the beans in a blender and mix them to a paste.) Put the bean paste into a clean, cloth-lined colander, and squeeze out the excess liquid by twisting the cloth tightly. Be careful not to make the paste completely dry.

The paste is now ready to use. Sugar and salt must be added before eating; the amounts are given in each recipe. This bean paste may be frozen for future use.
Makes approximately 2 cups

SAMPLE MENUS

SPRING

STEAMED EGG CUSTARD
Chawan Mushi

BAMBOO SHOOT RICE
Takenoko Meshi

RAW FISH
Sashimi

TERIYAKI SPARERIBS

GREEN ONIONS AND BABY CLAMS
Nuta

PICKLED VEGETABLES
Tsukemono

TEA

STRAWBERRIES

SUMMER

MISO SOUP
Miso Shiru

GREEN PEA RICE
Green Pea Gohan

TEMPURA

CUCUMBER AND NOODLE SALAD
Harusame Kyuri Namasu

PICKLED VEGETABLES
Tsukemono

TEA

MELON OR PEACH

AUTUMN

CLEAR SOUP
Suimono

CHESTNUT RICE
Kuri Gohan

CUCUMBER AND SEAWEED SALAD
Kyuri to Wakame Sunomono

SALT-BROILED FISH
Sakana Shioyaki

STIR-FRIED BURDOCK ROOT
Kimpira

PICKLED VEGETABLES
Tsukemono

TEA

PERSIMMON OR APPLE

WINTER

PLAIN RICE
Gohan

CHICKEN ONE-POT
Tori no Mizutaki

SPINACH WITH SESAME SEEDS
Horenso no Goma-ae

CHICKEN LIVERS TSUKUDANI
Tori no Kimo Tsukudani

PICKLED VEGETABLES
Tsukemono

TEA

MANDARIN ORANGE OR KIWI

GLOSSARY OF JAPANESE FOOD TERMS

ABURA Oil. For deep-frying or stir-frying, use pure vegetable, peanut or corn oil, or Oriental-style sesame-seed oil in small amounts, but never olive oil.
ABURAGE OR AGE Deep-fried soybean curd. Usually found in the refrigerator case in plastic bags of three to five golden-brown pieces.
AEMONO Mixed flavored foods.
AGAR AGAR See KANTEN.
AJI Spanish mackerel; also means taste.
AJINOMOTO Monosodium glutamate (MSG). A flavor enhancer that can be omitted from any recipe in this book without adversely affecting the result.
AKAMISO Red fermented soybean paste; somewhat saltier than *shiromiso,* the white variety. Usually packaged in plastic tubs or heavy-duty plastic bags; will keep refrigerated for up to one year.
AMANI Foods cooked with a sweet flavoring.

AMAZAKE Sweet *sake.*
AN Also known as *koshian* or *tsubushian;* paste made from *azuki* beans. Available in cans.
ARARE Rice crackers.
AWABI Abalone.
AWASE-ZU Seasoned vinegar.
AZUKI Small red beans. Available dried or cooked in cans.
BATAYAKI Fried in butter.
BENI SHOGA Pickled ginger root (page 161). Usually bright red; found whole, sliced or slivered in jars or plastic bags. Keep refrigerated when open.
BENTO Box lunch.
BUTA Pork.
CHAWAN MUSHI Steamed egg custard (page 30).
CHIKUWA Cylindrical *kamaboko.* Usually white, and grilled to a light brown.
CHIRASHIZUSHI Vinegared rice mixed with vegetables (page 120).
DAIKON Giant long white radish. Average length about 14 inches; white icicle radish may be substituted.
DAIKON OROSHI Grated white radish. Becomes soggy and slightly discolored if prepared too far in advance, but will keep well refrigerated in tightly covered container for about three hours.

DANGO Dumpling.

DASHI Basic soup stock. Usually made from *katsuobushi* and *dashi kombu;* available in instant forms as *dashi-no-moto* or *hon dashi* in granules, foil packets or large flow-through bags. See page 20.

DASHI KOMBU See KOMBU.

DONBURI "Big bowl." Also, a rice dish with various toppings. See pages 112 to 115.

EBI Shrimp.

EDAMAME Soybeans (page 151).

ENOKITAKE A species of edible mushroom with slender, whitish-yellow stems and tiny round caps. Usually found fresh with their clumpy, spongy roots (cut off before using), or canned; will keep fresh in refrigerator for about one week.

FU A feather-light cake made of wheat gluten. Comes dried in a variety of shapes and colors; becomes a little spongy when wet. Most commonly used as garnish in soup. To use, soak in lukewarm water for five to ten minutes, or until it expands, then gently squeeze out water.

FUKI Butterbur or coltsfoot plant. Recognizable as a long, fibrous green stalk. Will keep fresh in refrigerator for about one week; also available canned, packed in water. In most cases, celery can be substituted.

GOBO Burdock root. Slender roots of about 18 to 22 inches in length; usually found in stores in bundles of two or three unscrubbed and covered with dark brown loam. Can be stored as is in the refrigerator wrapped in plastic for about two weeks. To use, scrape clean with a dull knife or scrub brush, and immediately place in cold water to prevent discoloration. Also available canned.

GOHAN Cooked rice; also means meal.

GOMA Sesame seeds. Both black (see KUROGOMA) and white are used, the former stronger in flavor. To toast, place in a dry pan with lid over medium heat and toast until golden, shaking the pan constantly to prevent seeds from burning. To grind, place in a *suribachi* (Japanese mortar), and grind until flaky or a paste, depending on recipe.

GOMA ABURA Nutty-flavored oil made from sesame seeds. Do not confuse with sesame-seed oil sold in health-food stores, which has a much milder flavor.

GOMAME Small dried fish. Usually found in cellophane packages; store in airtight containers.

HAKUSAI Also known as *nappa*. Sold in most stores as Chinese cabbage, it is a pale green, cylindrical-shaped vegetable.

HARUSAME Thin, transparent noodles made from bean gelatin. Must be softened in water before using. *Harusame* translates to "spring rain."

HIYAMUGI Thin wheat noodle. Available dried; most often served cold.

HOKKIGAI Red clams. Found in stores fresh, frozen and canned.

HORENSO Japanese spinach. If unavailable, use young, tender Western spinach.

ICHIBAN DASHI Soup stock made from *katsuobushi* and *dashi kombu* (page 21).

ICHIMI Japanese chili powder. Available in cellophane packages.

IKA Squid.

IMO Potato.

INARI ZUSHI Also known as *age zushi*. Vinegared rice in a seasoned, fried soybean-curd (*aburage*) pouch (page 121).

IRIKO Small dried sardines. Usually found in cellophane packages; store in airtight containers.

ITO KOMBU Dried kelp in string form. Available in cellophane packages.

KABOCHA Japanese pumpkin (or squash). Small, ruddy and green skinned, with yellow-orange flesh; acorn squash or small pumpkin may be substituted.

KABU Turnip.

KAI Clam.

KAMABOKO

KAMABOKO Steamed fish-paste cake. Comes in various forms and colors; probably best recognized as rectangular-shaped white cakes, tinted red or green on the surface, resting on disposable wooden blocks and wrapped in plastic. Found in the refrigerator case. Often simply sliced and used as an hors d'oeuvre or garnish, or cooked in a number of dishes. Will keep refrigerated for about one week. See CHIKUWA.

KANPYO Dried gourd shavings. Long, sandy-colored strips; often used as a decorative tie-string or as a filling. Usually sold in cellophane packages. Before eating, soften in water and then gently knead with salt to increase absorbency. Rinse, and then boil until softened, adding seasoning as directed.

KANJAK Tuber-root flour or powder. Used for making *konnyaku* (page 52).

KANTEN Agar agar. A gelatinous product made from seaweed. Usually found in white, red or green filaments, or in powdered form. If unavailable, use conventional gelatin, although it is not recommended for use in recipes in this book.

KAPPA MAKI Vinegared rice with a cucumber center, rolled in *nori* (page 120).

KARASHI Dry, ground hot mustard. For best results, make a paste with very hot water in a small bowl, invert the bowl and let mustard ripen for about ten minutes. Substitute English dry mustard.

KASU Leftover.

KASUTERA Sponge cake (page 165).

KATAKURIKO Potato starch. Used as thickening agent and in batter for *tempura*.

KATSUOBUSHI Dried bonito. Most commonly used to make *dashi*; look like wood shavings. Available in cellophane packages and boxes.

KAZUNOKO Herring roe.

KIMPIRA Seasoned *gobo* dish (page 47).

KINAKO Ground roasted soybean flour. Light brown in color with a slightly nutty flavor; generally sold in six-ounce boxes.

KINISHI TAMAGO Finely sliced strips of fried egg. Used as garnish.

KINOME Bright green, tender leaves of prickly ash. Slightly minty in flavor; popular as garnish.

KINOME

KURI (CHESTNUTS)

KIRI-KOMBU Thin strips of *kombu*.

KOMBU Kelp. Dark green-brown in color, it is sold dried in large sheets, strips and other various cuts and sizes. *Dashi kombu* is the sheet form, an integral ingredient in the making of *dashi*. Before using larger pieces, wipe the *kombu* clean with a lightly dampened cloth, but never rinse with water or flavor will be lost. Some cooks also make slits on the edges of the *kombu* sheet so that the flavor is more easily released during cooking.

KOME Rice grain (uncooked).

KONNYAKU Also known as devil's tongue jelly. Gelatinous cake made from tuber-root flour; generally brown or gray in color; some cakes are flecked. Found fresh in the refrigerator case packaged in water in plastic tubs or sausagelike tubes, or can be made at home (page 52). If water is changed daily, will keep well in refrigerator for about two weeks. Before eating, gently rub with salt and parboil. Also available canned. See SHIRATAKI.

KOSHIAN Smooth paste made from *azuki* beans. Available canned or can be made at home (page 169). See TSUBUSHIAN.

KURI Chestnuts.

KUROGOMA Black sesame seeds. (See GOMA.) If unavailable, use black poppy seeds.

KYURI Cucumber. Japanese variety is smaller and more delicate in flavor than United States variety.

MAGURO Tuna.

MAKIZUSHI Vinegared rice rolled in sheets of *nori* (pages 117 to 119).

MANJU Sweet-rice cakes filled with *koshian*. Sold fresh and frozen in cellophane packages. Best purchased at *manju* specialty shops. Can also be made at home (pages 168 to 169).

MATSUTAKE Dark-brown mushrooms grown under pine (*matsu*) tree. Fresh *matsutake* is available in the Pacific Northwest, but most areas must be satisfied with canned.

MATTCHA Powdered green tea. Available in tins.

MIKAN Mandarin orange.

MIRIN Sweet rice wine (*sake*) used for cooking. If unavailable, substitute dry cooking sherry or *sake*, adding one teaspoon sugar for each tablespoon of *sake* used.

MISO Fermented soybean paste. See AKAMISO, SHIROMISO.

MISO SHIRU Soup made with *miso*.

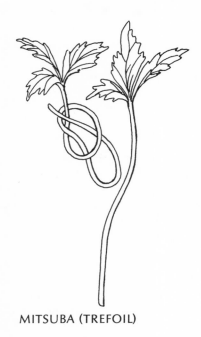
MITSUBA (TREFOIL)

MISO-YAKI Broiled food that has been seasoned with or marinated in *miso*.
MITSUBA Trefoil. A pale-green parsley.
MOCHI (O-MOCHI) Cakes made from sweet (glutinous) rice. Hot steamed sweet rice is pounded and shaped into flat, round cakes or sheets; available fresh or frozen wrapped in plastic.
MOCHIGOME Sweet (glutinous) rice. "Sticky" rice used to make *mochi*.
MOCHIKO Flour made from sweet (glutinous) rice. Usually sold in boxes or tubes.
MOMIJI OROSHI Grated *daikon* with red chili pepper.
MOYASHI Bean sprouts.
MSG Monosodium glutamate. See AJINOMOTO.
MUSHIMONO Steamed food.
MYOGA A type of Japanese ginger.
NAMASU Raw vegetable salad, usually with a vinegar-based dressing.
NAPPA Chinese cabbage. See HAKUSAI.
NASUBI Eggplant. Usually means the long, small Japanese variety.
NEGI Shallot. Green onion or leek can be substituted.
NERI *Miso* sauce.
NIBAN DASHI Soup stock made from second boiling of *dashi kombu* and *katsuobushi* reserved from making *ichiban dashi* (page 21).
NIGIRI (O-NIGIRI) Rice ball.
NIKU Meat.
NIMONO Simmered food.
NINJIN Carrots.

NIRA Garlic chives.
NISHIME Cooked vegetable dish.
NORI Sheets of dried laver. Usually dark green or blackish brown in color; generally sold in large sheets (eight by six and seven-eighths inches) folded in half in cellophane packages or tin boxes, or in smaller three-inch strips that are sometimes lightly seasoned (*ajitsuke-nori*). *Nori* can be found in several shapes and forms, from large sheets to crumbled, toasted and untoasted, plain and seasoned. Store in a dark place in an airtight container.
OBORO Dried shredded shrimp.
O-CHA Tea.
ODEN *Kamaboko,* meat and vegetables cooked in broth (page 103).
OKARA Residue remaining after making *tofu*. Looks like moist, fine sawdust. Usually found in Japanese food markets in large tins and sold in plastic bags by individual need; ask at the fish counter. Many stores give it to customers free. High in protein; can be

used in cooking for bulk and roughage. See page 51.

OKAYU Soft cooked rice (page 123).

OKAZU Foods that go with rice (pages 124 to 127).

OMANJU See MANJU.

O-MOCHI See MOCHI.

OROSHI Grated vegetable, usually *daikon*.

OYAKO DONBURI Large bowl of rice topped with cooked chicken and egg (page 112).

PANKO Japanese bread crumbs. Has appearance of white flakes; usually found in cellophane packages. Regular bread crumbs can be substituted.

PIMAN Small Japanese bell pepper.

PONZU Dipping sauce of lemon or vinegar and soy sauce.

RAKKYO Pickled scallions or shallots.

RENKON Lotus root. Resembles links of cream-colored potatoes; snowflakelike pattern when cut into rounds; crunchy texture. Store in dark, cool place, but use as soon as possible. Canned and dried forms are also available.

SABA Mackerel.

SAKANA Fish.

SAKE Japanese rice wine. Used in cooking and as a beverage.

SANBAIZU Sauce of sugar, soy sauce and vinegar.

SANSHO Pod of prickly ash. Greenish-brown spice with a "peppery" taste; sold in ground form in tin container.

SASHIMI Sliced raw fish.

SATO IMO Taro potato. Type of Japanese yam with a slightly gluey texture when cooked.

SAYA-ENDO Snow peas.

SENBEI Sweet crackers.

SHICHIMI TOGARASHI Spice mixture of red pepper, white sesame seeds, *nori,* mandarin peel, *sansho* and black hemp seeds. Generally sold in small tin containers.

SHIITAKE Dried black mushrooms. Must be softened in lukewarm water before use. Also available fresh in some markets.

SHIOYAKI Salt broiling. Rubbing salt into skin of fish (or chicken), then broiling. The salt assures a moist, flavorful result. See page 63.

SHIOZUKE Japanese salt pickles.

SHIRASUBOSHI Small dried white fish. Available in cellophane packages; store in airtight containers.

SHIRATAKI Yam noodles. *Konnyaku* in filament form; translates to "white waterfall." See KONNYAKU.

SHIRO-AE Vegetables with mashed *tofu* dressing.

SHIROMISO White fermented soybean paste. Considered sweeter than *akamiso,* the red variety. Usually packaged in plastic tubs or heavy-duty plastic bags; will keep refrigerated for up to one year.

SHISO Beefsteak or perilla plant, belonging to the mint family. Generally just the leaves, of which there are two kinds, green and red, are used. Green *shiso* is more frequently used as a garnish and spice, and sometimes as a vegetable in cooked dishes, such as *tempura*. In some cases, fresh spearmint or basil may be substituted. Red *shiso* is like the green in use, but is more often seen as the coloring for *umeboshi* (page 160). The plant's flowering seedpods are often used as a garnish and spice. Although *shiso* does not keep for very long, even refrigerated, some markets do carry it fresh, or parboiled in vacuum-sealed packs.

SHOGA Ginger root.

SHOYU Soy sauce. Made from soybeans, wheat and salt; two basic types—light and dark. Light soy sauce is just that— lighter in color and thinner, but saltier, and should be used sparingly as a seasoning that will not darken the color of the foods. Dark soy sauce being more full bodied is widely used as a daily table sauce and as a marinade.

SOBA Buckwheat noodles. Sold fresh and dried.

SHUNGIKU Edible chrysanthemum leaves. Usually parboiled briefly and served in salads; also good in *nabemono* dishes.

SOMEN Very thin wheat noodles. Sold dried.

SU Vinegar.

SUIMONO Clear soup (page 23). Instant forms are available.

SUKIYAKI Dish of beef cooked with vegetables (pages 96 to 97).

SUNOMONO Vegetable salad with vinegar-based dressing.

SUSHI Rice seasoned with sweetened vinegar. See pages 116 to 121.

TAI Sea bream.

TAKENOKO Bamboo shoot. Fibrous, crunchy texture with very little taste. Fresh, raw bamboo, which has several layers of brown husks, should be eaten immediately. To prepare for use, boil the shoot for about one to one and one-half hours, then immerse in cold water. Remove the husks. Canned boiled bamboo, with husks already removed, is also available, and should be rinsed thoroughly before using. Store fresh boiled and canned bamboo in tightly sealed container with fresh water to cover; will keep refrigerated for about one week.

TAKO Octopus.

TAKUWAN Pickled *daikon*. Usually yellow in color; found in jars, vacuum-sealed packs and sometimes in large tubs in various cuts and sizes. Keep refrigerated.

TAMAGO-YAKI Cooked egg.

TEKKA MAKI Vinegared rice with a tuna center, rolled in *nori* (page 120).

TEMPURA Seafood and vegetables deep-fried in light batter (pages 72 to 79).

TEPPAN YAKI Grilled vegetables and meat (page 81).

TERIYAKI Broiled meat, poultry or seafood that has been marinated in soy sauce-based marinade. (A more refined Japanese definition omits the marinating, and the sauce is simply brushed on the food as it is broiled.)

TOFU Fresh soybean curd. Several types are available, but the most common is blocks in small plastic tubs in the refrigerator case. Some brands will have a date stamped on the container, and the *tofu*, should be eaten within five to seven days of that date. Keep refrigerated in plenty of water; change the water daily.

TOGAN Winter melon. Large, green melon with powdery white film on surface. Commonly used for making soup.

TOGARASHI Small hot red chili pepper. Can be found fresh, but usually dried—whole or crushed.

TSUBUSHIAN Unstrained paste made from *azuki* beans. Available canned. See KOSHIAN.

TSUKEMONO Pickled vegetables; wide variety available in most stores, or can be made at home (pages 154 to 161).

TSUKUDANI Foods cooked in soy sauce and sugar for preserving. Usually found canned or vacuum-packed.

TSUYU Clear broth.

UDON Thick, white wheat noodles. Found fresh in the refrigerator case, frozen and dried in cellophane packages.

UMANI Chicken and vegetables cooked in seasoned broth (page 101).

UME Commonly known as a Japanese plum, it is a species of apricot.

UMEBOSHI Salty pickled plums *(ume)*. Most stores carry col-ored-red, pickled plums; will keep indefinitely. May also be made at home (page 160).

UNAGI Eel. Available frozen and broiled in cans.

UNI Sea urchin. Not commonly found fresh; readily available pickled in salt.

WAKAME Variety of leafy seaweed. Usually found in dried form in cellophane packages, or some Oriental markets store it in large jars.

WASABI Horseradish plant. The fresh root can be grated and used as a spicy garnish, but in the United States it is usually seen as a pale-green paste accompanying *sashimi*. Most stores carry the powdered form in small, round tin cans. For best results, mix the powder with cold water to a paste and let it stand,

covered with an inverted glass, for 10 minutes before using. Once the can has been open, store the powdered *wasabi* in the refrigerator.

YAKIMYOBAN Japanese alum.

YAKIMONO Grilled or pan-fried food.

YAKITORI Skewered chicken and vegetables grilled over a charcoal fire or in a broiler (page 144).

YOKAN Sweet made from gelatin and *azuki*-bean paste.

YOMOGI MOCHI Green cakes made from sweet (glutinous) rice. Hot steamed rice with crushed *yomogi* is pounded and formed into flat, round cakes. *Yomogi* is the name of the plant that gives it the green color.

YOSENABE "A gathering of everything." Seafood stew (page 95).

YUZU A Japanese citrus fruit. Small and yellow, it has use similar to that of lemon or lime. Most Japanese stores in the United States are beginning to carry this fruit.

MAIL-ORDER SOURCES

The following firms handle mail-order requests for canned and bottled ingredients and dried herbs and spices. You are advised to write to the firm nearest you and request information on the products available and shipping arrangements. Some firms have a minimum amount, such as $10, that must be ordered for fulfillment.

K. Tanaka Co. Inc.
326 Amsterdam Avenue
New York, NY 10023
(212) 874-6600

G.T. Sakai & Co.
1313 Broadway
Sacramento, CA 95818
(916) 446-7968

Yoshinoya
36 Prospect Street
Cambridge, MA 02139
(617) 491-8221

Anzen Pacific Imports
7750 N.E. 17th
P.O. 11407
Portland, OR 97211
(503) 283-1284

Uwajimaya
15555 N.E. 24th
Bellevue, WA 98007
(206) 747-9012

Uwajimaya
519 6th Avenue South
Seattle, WA 98104

Oriental Store of Raleigh
3121 North Boulevard
Kings Plaza Shopping Center
Raleigh, NC 27604
(919) 876-6911

INDEX

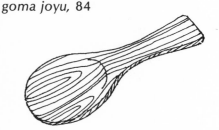

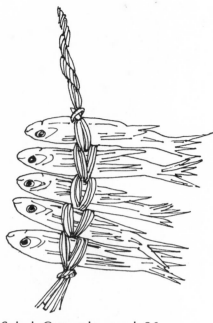

BIOGRAPHICAL NOTES

DELPHINE HIRASUNA and DIANE J. HIRASUNA are sisters whose grandparents emigrated from Japan to California in the early part of this century. Their family in Hiroshima have been master chefs catering banquets for three generations. Many of these chefs' culinary secrets were imparted to the Hirasuna sisters by their mother, who was taught to cook by her great uncle while she attended school in Japan. Many of the other recipes in this book were brought to this country by the authors' grandmother, who adapted the dishes to her evolving Americanized taste and the ingredients available in America.

Diane and Delphine Hirasuna were born and raised in Lodi, California. Diane has degrees in sociology and psychology from Sacramento State University and is currently employed as a workers' compensation counselor for northern California hospitals. Delphine has a degree in social science from San Francisco State University. A journalist for the past 15 years, she is presently employed as manager of corporate publications at Potlatch Corporation. In addition, she writes weekly feature columns for *Hokubei Mainichi* in San Francisco and *Rafu Shimpo* in Los Angeles. Both Hirasuna sisters have traveled extensively in Japan.

SALLY NOLL is a graduate of Boston University's School of Fine and Applied Art and also studied at Skowhegan School of Painting and Sculpture in Maine. She is presently a free-lance graphic designer in Berkeley, California, with work ranging from brochures to tapestry designs. Her most recent credits include Christmas cards for Cartier and, in 1979 and 1980, for the Museum of Modern Art in New York City.